And In The End

And In The End

The World's Weirdest Funerals

Keith R Lindsay

First published in 2006 by Fusion Press,
a division of Satin Publications Ltd
101 Southwark Street
London SE1 0JF
UK
info@visionpaperbacks.co.uk
www.visionpaperbacks.co.uk
Publisher: Sheena Dewan

A catalogue record for this book is available
from the British Library.

ISBN-13: 978-1-905745-00-5
ISBN-10: 1-905745-00-1

2 4 6 8 10 9 7 5 3 1

Cover photo: Lawrence Lawry/Getty Images
Cover and text design by ok?design
Printed and bound in the UK by Cox & Wyman Ltd,
Reading, Berkshire, RG30 3DL

To my wife Sue and my offspring Jamie and Hannah
for believing in my impossible, to John Bolton Evans just
because, and to my late father Bob, for giving me the
opportunity to work the room at a funeral service.

Contents

Acknowledgements

With thanks to my editor Louise for her patience, organisation and positivity, and John G Temple for pulling me back into the game. And to Guy Rose, my agent, to whom I'd also like to say thank y–, which is thank you minus his usual percentage.

Acknowledgements

Introduction

Let me reassure you – you are not sick, well not totally anyway. Yes, you have in your hot little hands a book on the subject of funerals, and yes, it's a book you're meant to find kind of fun and funny: but that doesn't make you sick. Seriously, who among us hasn't at some time laughed, or at least felt like laughing, at a funeral? And when I say laugh I mean anything from that sneaky snigger you try to disguise as a cough or sneeze, to the side-shaking explosion perfected by your Uncle Malcolm with the glass eye who works in litter enforcement. It's natural, it's normal; it's merely a release of tension. Unless, of course, you're attending the funeral of a total stranger with the express intention of laughing, in which case you are one sick puppy.

The book you are clutching is a trawl through the strangely amusing side of life's final journeys, from the rituals of the ancient world to the idiosyncrasies of modern man.

If I were writing a thesis I'd probably be discussing the recent and rapid change in purpose of the modern funeral, from paving the way for the deceased's journey to the afterworld to becoming more the celebration of a life lived. And in the course of accepting that, I'd ask you to remember that the greatest gift you can give anyone is the gift of laughter – though the gift of your body comes pretty damn close. I would also have to kick off by talking about how the world used to do funerals, from the ancient past to recent history, which strangely enough is exactly how the book begins. After all, if we want to understand how the modern funeral has become the fun fest it has, it's good to check out what our forefathers did. Besides, it's easier to laugh at the long dead than the more recently passed.

The ancients and not-so ancients did indeed have some strange, sometimes cringeworthy, funeral foibles, but make sure you read on to prevent any possible feeling of superiority – you'll see that with age there doesn't always come wisdom. And no matter how much the world of weeping has changed, there will always be certain elements of your average funeral that can be taken as standard. There's usually a body for a start, some sort of receptacle for it and a place for its final disposition. This book will take you through the multitude of options – from novelty coffins to cryogenic freezing – and will show you all the other essential, and non-essential, elements to the modern funeral. For instance, what used to be called the eulogy could now be classed as anything from a character assassination to a stand-up comedy routine, and the solemnity of the funeral hymn has given way to the happy-clappy harmonies of chart music. Even the final resting place has outgrown the boundaries of the churchyard – venturing as far as outer space.

Somewhere in the course of writing this book it occurred to me that it should be entirely up to you, the reader, to decide if what you were reading sounded funny or fun, and that those who wanted to might be inclined to read this volume as a kind of handbook for adding a little lightness into their own funeral or the funeral of someone they love. And you know what, I have no problem at all with that, you just go right ahead.

Now read on, because, as George Bernard Shaw said, 'Life does not cease to be funny when people die any more than it ceases to be serious when people laugh.'

Chapter 1

A Little Light History – Part I

One of the objectives of this little volume is to put the fun back into funerals. Now I know what you're thinking – it was never there in the first place. Wrong. It has always been there. Want some proof? Then let me transport you back to the dawn of man.

In that age before the wheel, the flame and the fridge magnet, man was very much kin with his neighbour, the wild beast. The concept 'funeral' did not exist; you died and were left to moulder where you fell, naturally or unnaturally. Assuming, of course, yours was not a cannibal tribe.

For millennia after we struggled out of the primordial ooze – and most likely even before we did so – when any creature died it either returned to the elements where it came to rest or, more likely, was devoured by those beasts who preyed on the recently deceased: vultures, crows, jackals, anything with sharp teeth and a strong constitution in fact. Obviously there had to be certain exceptions

4

to the rule. Somehow I can't imagine even primitive man being so truly primitive as to leave one of his own to simply return to the earth if he died in his sleep, especially if there was a primitive girlfriend involved. I'm thinking she'd definitely kick up a stink, as eventually would he.

Sleeping arrangements aside, there must have been other exceptions too: you wouldn't want to pollute your source of drinking water, would you? And what if one of your tribe keeled over while preparing lunch? He'd have to be tossed out of the tossed salad. (Unless, of course, you were actually cannibals.) There had to be plenty of other exceptions too, and thus, possibly as we became more civilised, their number grew until the exceptions became the rule.

And the rules? Obviously I wasn't there when they formed the committee, but I suspect they'd include burial away from food or drinking water and in fact outside the camp altogether due to the smell and risk of disease and hopefully out of the reach of inquisitive children – a five-year-old with a poking stick is a five-year-old with a poking stick no matter which millennium you're in.

The idea of universal burial seems to have taken a while to catch on worldwide; even as late as the 13th and 14th centuries the Mongols (Genghis Khan's lot) were still disposing of their dead the carrion way. They would tie the dead body to a horse and remove it from the immediate vicinity with a quick slap to the rump of the horse – like those cowboy movies where the Indian shot off his pony but has his foot caught in a stirrup and is dragged off into the distance.

However, though universal burial itself was not on the horizon, graveyards were. Legend has it that the mightiest of beasts, the elephant, knew when its terminal time was nigh and made its way slowly and sedately to its final resting place, its secret final resting place. The stories handed down to us tell of huge, secret or lost elephant graveyards where the bones and, more importantly for the legend, the ivory tusks shimmer into the distance. Yes the emphasis is on the word legend, but it's still something we humans could adopt – a special place in each country where ailing accountants, stamp collectors or white van drivers go to die. I suppose the closest we get to such a place today is the military graveyard; there is a commonality there, unlike the rest of us who find our peace beside the butcher, the baker or software manufacturer.

The Stone Age – first funerals

For the uninitiated, the Stone Age was basically divided into three periods as far as mankind goes: the Palaeolithic, Mesolithic and Neolithic. The Neolithic period being the final stage of the Stone Age, its Latin translation meaning new stones – unsurprising really since they'd probably worn out all the palaeo and meso ones over the years. The Age as a whole lasted from some 6,000 years BCE to approximately 1,700 years BCE. The move from one age to the other was somewhat gradual – stones are heavy you know – but basically as Stone Age man became master of rock, the bigger the rocks he could master.

So just when did we first start burying our dead with some sort of ceremony and not just for health and safety reasons? Well, according to archaeologists, at least 350,000 years ago. It seems while excavating a pre-Stone Age burial pit in Northern Spain the Indiana Joneses found an axe buried with the ancient remains. Now the archaelogists say this shows that those who interred him must have had some conception of an afterlife and believed he might need his tools when he got there – possibly theirs was an incomplete Heaven. Of course, while it may show that line of thinking, it may just as well have been some little Neanderthal boy who'd been given an axe for his birthday the same day they planted one of his relatives; 'I said stop playing with that axe! If you keep throwing it up and down … No, you can't climb in and get it!'

Thus maybe little Ug started a trend, because by the Neolithic period they were chucking stuff in after the body like it was going out of fashion. Which it may well have been;

you're not going to throw away this year's hot designer animal skin or the shawl your wife had copied from the ones they're all wearing this year down in the big hamlet.

As our ancestors grew more civilised so did their obsession with what have become known as grave goods. Neanderthal remains that were discovered in the Shanidar Caves in modern-day Iraq were found covered in pollen, which shows that the tradition of funeral flowers goes back at least 10,000 years or more. Archaeologists conclude that the freshly picked blooms may have been used to mask the smell of the decomposing corpse. So dead Stone Age man smelt worse than live Stone Age man. Who knew?

Soon burial and the funeral took on their own rituals; everyone wanted a path to this better place, this 'afterlife'. Graves became more than simple holes in the ground – the dead were dressed for the occasion, sometimes with a little body make-up made of lime wash, and the corpse was accompanied to the afterlife with many of his earthly possessions. But as in life so in death, and of course the rich were able to take more with them; their funeral pits and burial mounds had to be bigger, better, moundier. The common form of burial for the wealthy was a pit large enough to hold their remains and their luggage, covered by a large mound to mark the grave and remind everyone how powerful they were. The bigger the mound, the more

powerful the occupant – think rock stars' homes. The poor
had to settle for being stuffed into a cave with the family's
second-best serving bowl.

The rich 'can take it with you' list included pottery, flint
knives and bone pins. Grave goods as varied as antlers, axe
heads and jewellery have been excavated at Bogebakken,
in Denmark, where, as well as the usual practice of lime-
washing the bodies, archaeologists found evidence of face
painting with red ochre. It seems it wasn't enough to take
your favourite possessions with you to the nether world,
you had to go there looking like my Nan.

It's around this time in northern Europe, some 4,000 to
6,000 years ago, that a choice about how to go was introduced.
When I say choice – the deceased had little say in the matter; it
was more likely up to the surviving family members to decide
on cremation or inhumation. Inhumation being the cutting up
of the body into more manageable parts – a sort of kid's-meal
corpse. And although cremation has made a comeback over
the last century or so, inhumation is now mostly confined to
horror movies with 'part II' or 'III' in the title.

Choice was similarly to be had in your final resting place.
If you were rich or powerful (although I doubt there was
an 'or' involved) you had the choice of your ashes or bits
being interred in a passage tomb, a wedge tomb, a court
tomb or a portal tomb. For those wondering, the passage
tomb was an underground grave with – you guessed it – a

passage leading to it, the wedge tomb was a passage set into a wedge-shaped mound, the court tomb was a cairn or barrow (or lump in the ground) with a court of stones or earthworks encircling it, and the portal tomb a barrow with a portal consisting of three large stones covered by a huge monolithic slab, some of which could weigh up to 40 tons. So your Stone Age upper echelons were left with the basic choice of anything from a hole in the ground to a mono-lith-marked tomb. The slightly less rich and powerful had the same choice but were mostly forced to share; there are 1,500 such shared tombs in Ireland alone. And if you had no riches and no power at all: well, it's hard to tell how they were buried as they rarely had much to leave behind.

The Ancient Zoroastrians

Back in good old 2000 BCE, before Northern Europe was making its burn or butcher choice, a few thousand miles away, in what is now modern-day Iran, the Ancient Zoro-astrians were performing the ritual of Dakhma-Nashini: the 'utter destruction of the dead body'. And, in fact, this practice was so popular that it hung around until about 900 CE.

These Zoroastrians had real issues with the corpse, believing it to be evil and capable of polluting the living. Their rituals called for none but special corpse bearers to be allowed to touch the body, and for that honour they were forced to live away from the main town or village. They must have had a good pension scheme is all I can think.

The body had to be washed with the freshly collected urine of a special white bull. And if anyone other than the corpse bearers did somehow touch the body, and were thus powerless in mind, tongue and hand, then they too had to wash in the urine and even sip it to cleanse themselves inside and out.

The Zoroastrians then did the more common practice of prayers over the body, and allowed the family to say the final farewells, although this wasn't permitted if one of the family members was pregnant in case the prayers had an effect on the unborn soul. The body was then raised up on a pile or plateau to be devoured slowly by the sun and the local vultures, a practice shared by the Parsees – a more modern-day offshoot of the Zoroastrian religion in India. It was left to the wind and rain to decimate and drive the remaining bones into the sea. There's one beach that's going to struggle to get its blue flag.

The Bronze and Iron Ages

Back in Europe a couple of new ages dawned, and, much like us, the post-Stone Age peoples discovered two important concepts: recycling and quality over quantity.

And In The End

Whether they just became bored with building elaborate tombs for people who, let's face it, were not going to appreciate them, or some sort of local planning committee decided that yet another barrow would not be in keeping with the character of the area and would have an adverse effect on the price of the local roundhouses, we'll never know. For whatever reason, the practice of re-using previously loved barrows and wedge tombs became commonplace. What was left of the previous occupants was moved to a communal bone grave, the forerunner of the ossuary, before the new occupant was allowed to take possession.

The less-is-more concept was applied to the burial of grave goods; fewer items were interred with the remains but they were of higher quality – semi-precious jewels, weapons, bronze boxes, enamelled ware and stone and glass beads.

Towards the end of this era in north-west Europe, and in Denmark, Germany, the Netherlands, England and Ireland especially, a new form of burial – submergence in a peat bog – became popular, if not with the victim. I say victim, as this was not for those who died a natural death, but was for those selected for human sacrifice or brutal punishment. These people were subject to horribly painful deaths: garrotting, having their skulls caved in with a hammer, being drowned in brown slimy bog water, all after being extensively tortured (they took great pleasure in the slicing off of the nipples apparently), but let's look on the bright side – wet peat is really good for the skin.

The Pagans of northern Europe were possibly the first to come up with the idea of funeral clothes. They believed that if the body was dressed for death in new clothes the evil spirits wouldn't recognise the soul of the deceased and he could escape to whichever afterlife they believed in unmolested. I've watched enough scary movies to know that evil spirits probably are that dumb.

The Vikings

The last great age of grave goods in the Western world was the era of the Viking. Spreading terror and trade in equal measure from their homelands in Scandinavia, the Norsemen also seem to have turned the flashy funeral into an art.

Again this was restricted to the influential, the distinguished and the famous – basically anyone who would have been in the pages of a Viking celebrity gossip magazine. And even then there was a hierarchy within those ranks.

The Viking C-list celebrity would be buried in their finest garments with their weapons, jewels and food and drink for their life in Valhalla (the Viking version of Heaven) placed beside them, whereas the Viking George Clooney would be cremated in his longship, with all of the above but also with his Thor Hammer, his dog, his horses and sundry other animals. In early pagan Viking times there may even have been a human sacrifice.

Those who were buried were done so with coffins constructed to the size needed to fit the deceased and all he was taking with him – and sometimes this included his horse. Of course, it was only the men who had the huge celebratory funerals. Viking women's coffins tended to be smaller and their grave goods were confined to the more refined items such as necklaces and beads.

The Ancient Egyptians

The Egyptian version of the afterlife was much like their former life, only without so much sand. They believed that since they would exist in much the same way as they were alive, they would need their bodies to be preserved as close as possible to their pre-death state – although that's a pretty loose definition if it means being wrapped from head to toe in linen with the inner bits of you removed and put in a jar by your side.

A Little Light History – Part I

Naturally, this famous practice of mummification was confined to the powerful and rich Egyptians, as only they were deemed worthy of having their bodies in their next lives.

Embalming the bodies was a complex business. First, the body was purified by washing and shaving. Then they cut open the body and removed all the internal organs, except the heart – the apparent location of intellect and memory. This even included the brain, which was often removed through the nose by means of a hook. Then, once the insides were out, linen pads and sawdust took their place and the body was covered with sodium bicarbonate to dry out the body. After two months of follow-up cleaning and anointing, the body was finally wrapped with linen and ready to scare the willies out of anyone from Abbott and Costello to Brendon Fraser.

After mummification these King Tutankhamens and Queen Cleopatras were laid to rest in their bespoke pyramids, with their treasured objects ready for use in the next life, including the book of the dead, their own version of a Rough Guide to the Afterworld. And yes we're talking about the high and mighty in human and pyramid terms, since obviously not everyone could afford the 2,000–5,000 men, or 100,000 slaves according to the Greek historian Herodotus, and the 25 years required to complete such a monumental structure. Yes 25 years! They must have used the same builders who still haven't managed to complete my bathroom extension.

However, the dead didn't always get to the afterlife as quickly as they thought. Sometimes mummies were kept above ground for years and used as loan collateral. A variation of this actually turned up again in Scotland many centuries later when it wasn't unheard of for the corpse of someone with unpaid bills to be taken into custody until they were settled.

If you've been paying attention you may have spotted what you see as a major flaw in Egyptian logic: you're thinking if only the powerful were mummified, and only the mummified moved on to the next life, how were they going to cope without their slaves and servants? Simple – they took them with them, sealed up alive in the tomb.

The Ancient Greeks

The Ancient Greeks are considered men of culture, as the fathers of drama, philosophy, democracy – and the home burial. They believed death meant eternity in Hades and that the dead had to cross the River Styx by ferry to get there. They even placed a copper coin on the tongue of the deceased in order to pay the ferryman.

Before they became totally civilised the ancient Ancient Greeks (from around 500 BCE) would build rooms in their own homes for the express purpose of burying the bodies of their dead. So an estate agent's particulars for a lovely

Athenian semi-detached just on the market would be likely to read: 'Three beds, modernised kitchen, lounge/diner, vendor willing to leave rugs, murals and grandma.'

The effect on the housing market might account for the Greek movement to burying their dead on deserted islands – though they'd probably have to check first that the islands were truly deserted and it wasn't merely out of tourist season.

The Greeks were possibly among the first to perform some sort of ritualised wake for the dead, the *prothesis*, whereby the dead were washed, oiled and laid out on a high bed ready for the arrival of friends and relatives who'd come to pay their respects, and do a little weeping and moaning – mostly about the fact they couldn't see the body because the bed was too high.

In common with the Egyptians, the Greeks also had a love of decorating their graves or tombs with pictures. Though, unlike the Egyptians who preferred images of their gods, the Greek reliefs were lifelike representations of the occupier, perhaps with his servants, possessions and sometimes the family pet.

The Ancient Romans

Ever sensible, the Romans prepared for their funerals far in advance. Those who could afford to, built their own tombs in their lifetimes, or more correctly had them built for them. The less affluent, though spared the nightmare of having the builders in, were more likely to have their ashes interred in urns placed in niches cut into the walls in what became known as *columbaria*, because of their resemblance to a pigeon house or dovecote. If they'd been prudent they'd have joined the local *collegia funeralicia*, an ancient Co-operative funeral society, whereby paying their subs they could look forward to a decent funeral and a bit of divvy.

We get the word funeral from the Roman *funeralis* – a funeral torch that was ever-present at their processions.

Since the Romans insisted that all human remains were disposed of outside the city, funerals were obliged to march at night to the tomb or pyre. And if you're going to process then why not really go for it? It was led by the eldest son, who had to display his grief by having his hair dishevelled. Family and friends wore masks bearing the images of the family's forebears and the procession itself was headed by acrobats, jugglers, dancers and mimes. The procession was also liberally scattered with professional female mourners, whose weeping and wailing and beating of the breasts was in direct proportion to their pay cheque.

But the classical Roman funeral didn't end with the burning or burial, oh no. For nine days and nights after the funeral the house of the recently departed was supposed to be tainted. So on the ninth day they swept the house to brush out the ghost.

Actually it was probably just a further excuse for the Romans to have yet another feast; and boy were there many Roman holidays commemorating their ancestors. Among others were the *Parentalia* – a feast in honour of one's dead parents – and the *Lemuria* – when ghosts roamed abroad in May and it was up to the eldest son to try to appease them by offering them beans. Yes, no need for proton packs, exorcisms or tiny women with silly voices, just a handful of beans or a broom!

Top ten gruesome funeral facts from the past

1. Part of the Roman death ritual meant the eldest surviving male of the household had to rush to the deathbed to try to inhale his dying parent's last breath. Then, finally breathless, the body was washed in hot oil and water for seven consecutive days, though

I'm thinking the son might have taken a little longer trying to wash out his sinuses.

2. The Persians, Syrians and Babylonians made huge candles out of their dead. They kept the bodies of their dead in person-sized jars full of wax or honey, but it only needed a wick, right?

3. The Calations (or Carthaginians) were said to have eaten their own dead. They were a little picky about it though – only family members were allowed to partake, in fact it was their sacred duty. It was probably the one time the kids would actually rather eat their greens.

4. In Imperial Japan, a noble man could expect a goodly number of his slaves to commit suicide, or hara kiri, when he left this mortal coil. And it was even tougher for their Fijian counterparts as the dead man's slaves and his wives were strangled.

5. The Thais practised cremation but with a twist if you were royal, since the succeeding king had to sift through the ashes of his predecessor for bits of bone as symbols of his new authority.

6. The Choctaw Indians used to ripen the bodies of their dead by raising them above ground on a platform on posts or in a tree. This allowed the elements to do their work until the flesh was gooey enough to remove. What material was left on the bones was removed by use of the especially long and hardened fingernail of specially

employed bone pickers, who scraped off the rotting flesh, sinew and tendon until the bones were smooth and ready for the funeral, where they were placed in a soil and stone mound.

7. The Haitians once smoke-cured their dead and hung them from the walls of their houses like ornaments. Thus instead of family heirlooms, your heirlooms were your family, which in the case of certain South American tribes that meant jewellery made from their bones.

8. In certain arctic and sub-arctic areas, the prehistoric practice of simply leaving the body to its own devices was alive and well long after the world became merely historic. Well, you try digging a grave in permafrost.

9. In Central Asia the old Mongol method of letting the wild things chomp on the body transmuted into them keeping their own hairy funeral directors called dogs to devour the meaty morsels after inhumation.

10. On the Indian sub-continent they had their own little funeral peccadillo, until the British Colonial powers put a stop to it. Certain Hindus practised 'suttee', or – to put it bluntly – wife burning. As the deceased wouldn't be able to live without his wife after death, the widow was either expected to lie down next to her dead husband on his funeral pyre, or (as was more likely) was thrown on. Apparently not everyone was too upset by the banning of the practice.

Chapter 2

A Little Light History – Part II

The Middle Ages

From the Florentine peasant to the Bishop of York, the growing population of the medieval world were totally obsessed with death and the funeral. And it was a Europe-wide obsession that can probably be all put down to one thing – Purgatory.

The medieval Christian Church seems to have decided that Hell simply wasn't enough to keep the congregation in line, and the Church in donations. If you were a gambling man then Heaven or Hell was a 50/50 chance (though of course being a gambling man you were unlikely to be allowed the upper tier option). But if you still believed the weight of your good deeds tipped the balance in your favour, then why worry?

This is where the new wrinkle of Purgatory came in. It added a middle layer of management requiring even those on the Heaven side of the balance to pay for their sins.

Basically, they will let you go upstairs but will first do nasty things to you in the basement because you lied, cheated, coveted your neighbour's ox and wife, that sort of stuff. It wasn't as simple as a punishment per sin, though. There was a tariff, and the worse your sins in life the longer and more painful your stay in Purgatory.

So what has this to do with funerals? Well, the purpose of Purgatory wasn't simply to scare the people into being pious, it was a nice little earner too. It worked something like this: the fact that you were going to Purgatory was a given, but the length of time you spent there and the length of your scrotum when you finally left were negotiable. By doing a little repenting of your sins, living a good life and making a *bona mors*, or good death, you could earn a sizeable remission to your sentence. A good death obviously included the funeral; they even had a Teach Yourself Pious Endings book called the *Ars Moriendi* (the Art of Dying).

So, bluntly, the more spectacular the funeral the shorter your stay in you-know-where, and thus the penchant for three-day funerals. Once again the rich had the advantage – after all, spectacle costs. First there was the death announcement. This was not so much an ad in the local paper as the hiring of criers to ride 10 to 15 kilometres in every direction spreading the news 'the old Duke has popped his clogs!' In Brittany, France, four men, two women and two barefoot orphans would wander around the town ringing a bell and calling the inhabitants out to the funeral, and in Scotland and England someone called a 'bidder' would knock on your door to bid you attend the ceremonies, possibly with an 'or else'.

For three days before the service the body was kept in the deceased's own house watched over by paid mourners, again accruing more expense. This was apparently a necessary measure to make sure the sneaky beggar was really dead – they'd obviously been caught out that way before. This three-day waiting time could be shortened, however, due to mitigating circumstances, such as the smell.

In both England and Ireland the mourners or corpse watchers of some of the less powerful dead (you wouldn't dare take liberties with corpses whose relatives could have bits of you lopped off) seem to have come up with an amusing way of passing the lonely night hours; they liked to mess about a bit with their charge, imitating the deceased's voice and calling to the family. They would tie string to bits of the body and wave the limbs about; all good clean fun, guaranteed to scare the life out of the still living.

Smell notwithstanding, the vigil was followed by a procession in which all the locals were invited to take part. Of course, taking part meant they'd all need expensive torches and banners. It's said that the Duke of Burgundy ordered 1,500 black cloth bales to dress mourners for his funeral in the city of Bruges. The mourners were allowed to keep their new clothes afterwards, so it probably meant that that century's new black was actually black.

Possibly the most expensive ingredients of the medieval funeral were the prayers. After all, prayers were meant to be a direct line to God, and asking nicely for a little forgiveness for others went a long way. But, naturally, no one ever gets something for nothing and when it came to having a chat on your behalf with the Almighty, money talked.

And finally there was some good news for the poor since their prayers were apparently worth more remission when the decedent faced the Purgatory parole board. For their service they were given alms – food, money, shoes and clothes, you know, life's little extras. Plus, it was possible to cut down on the expense of your funeral a little by leaving your own beehives to the church in order to make the necessary funeral candles. But I guess you were stung either way.

Of course the poor weren't the only ones in on the prayer franchise; the major shareholders were the Church and they were not going to be bought off with food, shoes or clothes. In fact the fear of the flames led many people to leave their entire estates to the Church in return for prayers and masses. The number of prayers could reach into the thousands, until the money ran out that is. Some of the dying even indulged in a little spread betting by paying for the prayer services of several churches simultaneously. As I said, a nice little earner.

We can't leave the Middle Ages without a quick mention of their grave habits. The poor were buried in open pits or common graves with simple wooden crosses to mark their passing, and even the rich had to accept that once they had mouldered to bones they could expect to be asked to politely move on to the local charnel house. However, there were a few exceptions – and these were the medieval mega rich.

They say if you got it flaunt it, and for those in Switzerland, Italy, France, Belgium and England that meant huge stone tombs with life-size effigies of the deceased Duke-this or Lord-that carved onto their lids. The recumbent figure was often to be seen holding some token of their status or calling, such as swords for knights, crosses for the clergy and garlic presses for celebrity chefs.

Towards the end of the era a new form of tomb became fashionable. You know how it is, once something new has been on those tomb makeover shows everyone wants one. The Transi tomb, such as the one at the church of St Etienne at Bar-le-Duc in France, was not adorned with the figure of the tomb's host as such but had as its cover a carved decomposing corpse, with shards of flesh dripping from its bones and its insides providing munchies for worms.

Want to move on? Yes, me too.

The Renaissance

What can I say about the Renaissance funeral except, boy did they like the sound of their own voices? By this time the *Ars Moriendi* had become more of a handbook for life than for death and the funeral service had been appended with the funeral oration where the priests hammered and hammered the point home concerning how to live your corporal life in order to achieve eternal afterlife. From Lyon to Vilnius in Lithuania, these priests were the natural forerunners of the cable channel ministries bringing their Lord into your living room today.

The class divide in the funeral format continued to widen, just as it had done for many centuries, if not millennia. In England the poor were finally provided with an alternative to the home or church version. From Shakespeare's time onwards it became the done thing for those who couldn't afford the bells and wimples of a religious service to pop down to the pub. Taverns and inns offered a full funeral, complete with service, food and, strangely enough, ale. In some cases the inn was close enough to the local burial pit to even offer to dispose of the guest of honour at chucking out time – literally.

There was to be a minor glitch in the funeral poverty gap, however, with the untimely arrival of the Black Death. Since the disease showed no preference for rich or poor all were invited to bring out their dead to find equality of a kind on the funeral pyre or in the lime pit. It's during this time that the tradition of graves being six feet deep came into being with a law passed by the English. The idea was to bury a man deep enough to have his wife interred over him and still leave enough earth above to prevent any noxious stuff getting out. Just a pity the poor guy had to be dead to finally get his wife to go on top.

The 19th century

If we're coming to the end of our time travels, what better place to leap into than the last great age of mourning, the 19th century? And if we're going to take a look-see at funerals in the 19th century we're mostly going to be checking out the Brits.

So these were the rules. (Yes, in Victorian Britain you had to have rules, even in death. After all, you just simply couldn't have folk dying and doing all that other funeral-related stuff just where and how they felt like it now, could you?) Firstly, if you were a 19th-century stiff you weren't allowed to leave the house until your funeral. It was your duty to be laid out in the family home's parlour so that all those relatives who couldn't be bothered to visit while you were alive could come round to say how much they miss you now you're stiff as a board.

A Little Light History – Part II

Of course the poor didn't necessarily have a parlour so they were obliged to lay out their dead wherever they were able. And if that meant little Albert and his brothers having to share a bedroom with dead Daddy then so be it. In the US, funeral biscuits were handed out to those who came to view the body, wherever it happened to be displayed, though probably after they'd removed the kid's toys from Daddy's chest.

The rise of the undertaker or funeral director towards the end of the 19th century meant that this became the last great era of the home funeral. That said, the practice of saying goodbye to the deceased as they lay in the best room clung on in some communities in the UK until at least the 1960s. I remember my own grandfather receiving visitors in just such a manner. I recollect the comings and goings, the tears and the sniffles, though I wasn't actually allowed in to see his body. To this day I'm still not sure if it was simply because I was deemed too young or because I'd recently been bought a selection of watercolour paints. You make one dozy aunt look like Charlie the Clown while she's sleeping and you're branded for life!

Rule number two was that the whole house was deemed to be in mourning, and that even included the bricks and mortar. Black curtains were to be hung if you owned them, but if not the curtains you had were to be kept closed for the duration. In addition all mirrors were to be covered and clocks stopped at the exact time of death. The clock and mirror obsession isn't just a British trait, examples can be found across much of Eastern Europe as far as the Caucases. The entire close family had to wear black and those in society were obliged to send out invitations to the funeral on black-bordered cards. In France the invitation, the *faire part*, was sent to everyone even vaguely known to the family to notify them of the death.

Now, when the good Victorian mourners weren't busy showing visitors in and out of the parlour there was still plenty for them to do to show their grief. Post-mortem hair cutting was very popular. The Victorians considered hair to represent eternity since it appeared to grow after death. (Yes, I know it doesn't, it's just the skin on the skull shrinking, which makes it look like it's growing. Award yourself five points if you knew, though shame on you if you still believed.) The locks of hair were snipped from the dead bodies' heads and trapped in lockets, brooches or rings as a memento. Other harvested hair was used to make wreaths or hearts and enclosed in shadow boxes. Any curls left over were frequently passed out to the funeral guests.

The sending of locks of hair to relatives too distant to attend the funeral was especially popular in Australia. Unsurprising really, it's a huge hot country, and if you had to wait for some members of the funeral party to travel from Wollogorang to Wagga Wagga, well, let's just say there probably wasn't much left to bury.

In other parts of the world, Greece, Rome and Egypt, the hair of the widow or widower was cut off as a sign of mourning; in some cases this was to make them less attractive and thus off the market until the mourning period was over (or until they found someone who had a thing for bald heads).

So if they'd given the dear departed a short back and sides and still had two days to go to the big event, what else was there to do? Well, they could take a moment to make an equally personal memento – a death mask. They simply covered the face in liquid wax or plaster, allowed to dry, removed it and there they had a mould from which to cast a likeness of their late lamented loved ones.

Of course death masks were not new to the 19th century, but boy did they become popular. It seems anyone one who was a dead anyone simply had to have a death mask: Napoleon Bonaparte, Franz Liszt, Frédéric Chopin, Leo Tolstoy, Ludwig van Beethoven, Victor Hugo, Friedrich Nietzsche, Ned Kelly, the list just goes on. And it was a world-wide phenomenon, popular from Germany to Italy, from Russia to the US and all stations in between.

And In The End

The practice of death masks didn't simply die out with the 19th century. The likes of Alfred Hitchcock and even recent passers-on as Bruce Lee, Peter Lorre and Vincent Price, all have had them made.

There were various uses for the death mask; you could use them to commission a memorial portrait of the deceased, wait until both Grandma and Grandpa had died then use them as bookends or simply jump out from behind a door wearing them and scare the bejeezus out of little children.

While post-mortem portraits were the most popular use for the death mask, not everyone could afford to have such an expensive likeness of their loved one. Which is where the French and the new-fangled photography came in. The process of making multiple prints from one photograph allowed the French to send copies of the final picture to far-off relatives. The idea soon spread as a much cheaper alternative to the costly portraits. The dead were mostly photographed as if they were sleeping, though some families asked for their loved ones to be captured in still-life poses; Daddy hailing a handsome cab, Daddy smoking his meerschaum, Daddy chasing the maid around the scullery.

A Little Light History – Part II

Once the departed was hairless, had had his photograph taken and a mask of his final features made, it was time to dress him up in his best suit, or her finest white robe and cap, and deposit him in his silver-plate-handled, black-lined coffin. Only then was it time for the living to get ready for the main event.

Which brings us to rule three: funeral goers could wear any colour they liked as long as it was black. And that meant everything: black hair accessories, black umbrellas, black fans and purses, black dresses, hats, shawls, petticoats, black underwear, black lacy underwear, black see-through lacy underwear ... Actually silk crêpe was the preferred mourning material, while furs, satin and silk were forbidden as too decadent for death.

Men were allowed to wear their normal everyday attire, though don't think jeans and T-shirts with 'I'm with the stiff' on, as normal meant formal. Attendance at a funeral simply meant adding a black hat and/or gloves to your best, probably black, suit.

Perversely, white often replaced black for a child's funeral. I suppose black wasn't the only colour material in stock.

Funeral attire shops spread the length and breadth of the Britain to cater for the extravagance necessary to put on a good show. They were stocked to their high Victorian ceilings with everything from shoes to chapeaux. In Australia they took a much more pragmatic approach and encouraged the recycling and adapting of old dresses and accessories. And just in case the Old Country considered taking the colonial lead in this, it became considered unlucky to keep crêpe in the house after the mourning period, thereby guaranteeing the re-purchasing of another entire wardrobe of funeral wear the next time a family member passed on. And who considered it unlucky? The owners of the funeral attire shops maybe?

The funeral itself ranged from a priest at the side of a pauper's pit, to the plumed horses, ushers and army of mourners at the mausoleum of some Merchant Banker. In the good old Roman manner mutes or professional mourners could be hired to follow the procession and weep and wail in appropriate measure during the service, if you could afford them of course. The cheaper ones only managed a sniffle.

Even after the funeral there were still rules – mourning rules. The Victorians figured that if time was a healer and time could be measured, then mourning could be timed. And although there were many and various lengths of time for the living to mourn the dead depending on the social commentator, the average seems to have been a year and a day for a widow to mourn her husband and three months for a man who had lost his wife before he could get back out there.

If the widow and widower were top of the mourning tree then there was a sliding scale for all other family members to do their duty of sorrow. The loss of a mother or father also had a 12-month tariff, though you were let off with the veil.

A Little Light History – Part II

The mourning of children for their parents seems to have been around nine months, and, intentional or not, it does have a certain symmetry don't you think? All other close relations; brother, sister, step-whoever, grandparent, came in on the six-month mark. After that is was probably on downwards, from say a first cousin requiring maybe a month or so to the kid you once had to your fifth birthday party getting an 'oh well'.

And, much to the joy of the funeral attire shops no doubt, rules also applied to mourning wear. A widow was expected to wear black for the first six months of mourning, followed by grey and eventually lavender in her months of half mourning. Yes, half mourning. To wear anything brighter or, horror or horrors, figure flattering was immoral. I suppose it also helped keep the local rich widow hunters up to date with the countdown till they could pounce. Leaving the Brits aside for a moment, it should be said that it was quite common, and still is among traditionalists, in various Mediterranean countries for a widow to dress in black for the remainder of her life. (Well, at least you couldn't accuse them of spending hours trying to decide what to wear with their new shoes.) And in China the death of a parent once meant that a son was required to wear white for three years.

Back in Britain the mourning period usually meant that the widow could kiss goodbye to any social life except for attending church. Some corners of society even frowned upon the poor woman leaving her house to attend her husband's funeral. Nor was she allowed visitors of any description for the first month of widowhood. The widower, however, was expected to get on with his daily life and marry again as quickly as possible for the kiddies.

And yes, it all does seem a little prescriptive, but it has to be put in context; in previous centuries the widow could quite well have been expected to retire to a nunnery. And in regions of ancient China it was decreed that any marriage ceremony taking place within the mourning period was not only null and void but also earned the participants a beating. Twelve months doesn't seem quite so bad now, does it?

Thankfully the rest of the world was not quite so regimented in their funeral practices as the Victorians.

Top ten ideas we might consider resurrecting from funerals gone by

1. *Little black dresses:* Maybe we should consider bringing back mourning clothes, at least for the ladies. No, hear me out, for one thing you know you look good in black, it's figure flattering after all, and for another it would save you the dreadful decision over what to wear for the next 12 months after hubby has died and hence the possible embarrassment of being branded the Merry Widow.

2. *Grave goods:* I know some of you intend to sneak a little something into the coffin with you (though if you're British the law requires that it be made of natural, combustible/biodegradable materials only). But wouldn't it be cool to allow a much larger selection of grave goods, like in the good old Viking days? If they could be buried with their ships, why can't we be buried with our cars? It seems a fitting end to me, though there are one or two cars I've owned that deserve to be buried long before I meet my maker.

3. *The Viking funeral:* Why not bring back the whole Viking funeral? You know the one I mean, where Kirk Douglas is floated out into the sea on his longship and they fire lighted arrows into the sails so that the corpse drifts into the sunset in flames.

4. *Professional mourners:* I shouldn't need to sell you this one too hard; which of you doesn't like the idea of a crowd of young, attractive members of the opposite sex attending your funeral and weeping copiously? It'll certainly get the real guests talking!

5. *Suttee:* The ancient tradition of wife burning. Just think, with one fell swoop you'd instantly put an end to certain young healthy glamour models marrying old ailing millionaires.

6. *Community coffins:* There was a time when coffin-making materials were so scarce that the whole community

would contribute a little something to help. Though, come to think of it, if we tried that today you'd end up with a box made out of some left-over MDF, a couple of book shelves and the door off an old wardrobe some-one was always meaning to take to the tip.

7. *Giving it all away:* We could reprise the Victorian idea of handing out locks of hair to the mourners. In fact why not take it one step further and give away all the other bits of the body and dispense with the funeral altogether?

8. *Giving it all away II:* The indigenous peoples of the Canadian Interior would burn all the clothes and pos-sessions not already willed away by the deceased. And why, you may be asking, should we bring it back? Well, it's perhaps a less drastic version of number 5.

9. *Hit the road:* In Ancient Greece and in some northern European countries it was the practice for a brief time to bury the dead at the roadside. Well, it would give the kids a new game to play on those long car journeys.

10. *Sharing:* There was a time when the poor were required to share their bed with the dead whilst they were laid out for the wake. I don't see why we couldn't bring it back; after all some of us feel we've been sleeping next to a corpse for years.

Chapter 3

A Brief History of Being Buried Before Your Time

This chapter is all about those funerals where, technically, there wasn't a deceased. Or to get all Edgar Allen Poe about it – they were BURIED ALIVE!

The fear of being accidentally interred while there's still life in us is one of humanity's oldest nightmares; it ranks right up there with those dreams about being naked in class, forced dentistry and waking up to find you've metamorphosed into a creature with the body of reptile and the head of a perfume counter assistant. This paranoia seems to stretch back at least as far as records have been kept. One of the first recorded instances of accidental premature burial is apparently that of a member of St Columba's band of monks on the Isle of Iona. And how's this for unfair? He survived his interment for a whole night only to be put to death for heresy after he was dug up because he said he'd seen Heaven and Hell while he was down there.

Obviously it helps with your resurrection if you don't quite make it as far your dirt nap, as was the case with one

Matthew Wall in the 1500s. His pall-bearers dropped his coffin, allowing him to come to, live for several more years and party on his 'anniversary' in each of his extra years.

In the following century it also seems to have helped your disinterment if you took to the grave with you something worth stealing, and if your name was Marjorie. Both Marjorie Erskine and Marjorie Elphinstone were saved by the timely shovels of potential grave robbers: Marjorie One's groans scared the life out of her assailants, and back into herself. She walked home and outlived her 'widower' husband by six years. Marjorie Two, though, can probably outdo that; she returned to the world and promptly bore two sons.

In more recent times the Reverend Schwartz asked for his favourite hymn to be sung at his funeral and was then heard singing along from inside the coffin, and apparently the Bishop of the Greek island of Lesbos spent two days lying in state before asking one of the mourners filing past him what they were queuing for.

Of course, these people were the lucky ones (except for the Iona monk). They lived to tell the tale, and no doubt endlessly. Others were not so lucky, many others it seems. Although we only have evidence long after the fact, as it were. In South Carolina the skeleton of a girl was found out of her coffin and behind the door of her mausoleum. And when the time came for Thomas à Kempis to be transferred to the ossuary, they found scratches on the lid of his coffin.

This actually cost him a sainthood for not accepting his deliverance to God a bit early. Then there was the New Yorker interred in a temporary vault 120 years ago. When the time came to transfer her to more permanent accommodation, she was found to be several fingers short of a handshake in an attempt to keep her strength up until help arrived. And even more horrifying is the poor unfortunate Neapolitan woman from Italy. When her tomb was opened to give her some company, she was found with her clothes in shreds and that she had shattered every bone in her arms and legs in her final hysterical struggle to move the heavy tomb lid.

You're probably wondering how our forebears could get it quite so wrong, quite so often, and more worryingly if it could happen to you. But relax. If you're not dead already then getting yourself embalmed as part of your final rites should pretty well do for you. Or, to quote an Australian pamphlet from around 1900, 'Cremation eliminates all danger of being buried alive.' Thankfully the advertising slogan has come on a little since then.

The Victorians, and those who jumped the gun before them it seems, were frequently fooled by comas, the plague, smallpox, and, most commonly, catalepsy or cholera, any of which might render the body motionless and apparently breathless. And given the highly contagious nature of cholera you can understand why they might have been a little overanxious to plant the victim.

So mistakes happened, and this was possibly not helped by the fact that doctors didn't necessarily have to view the body to pronounce death. In some cases the family of the deceased merely needed to inform the doctor of death in order to obtain a certificate. It's just as well we no longer allow the calling in of death, because if lack of movement, lack of reaction and simply looking like death were the common criteria for obtaining a certificate then a hell of a lot of teenagers would be at risk of being buried alive.

So which age do you think was the time of mass 'buried alive' hysteria? Yes, you guessed it, the 1900s. And people went to really extreme lengths to make sure the ultimate nightmare didn't happen to them. The minimum requirement was a full set of instructions to 'check thoroughly' that they were dead before the burial. These included the odd little cut somewhere painful but not fatal (it would be kind of pointless otherwise), and the application of red hot irons and/or boiling water tipped over a section of exposed skin to check for any reaction. I'm guessing a piercing scream accompanied by a stream of expletives probably meant you were alive.

The fear was so strong that many had just such instructions as these written into their wills. I'm not so sure I'd trust a lawyer in such circumstances; 'Now sir, you may very well be alive, but I can't actually commission anyone to test if such be the case as per instructions contained in your last will and testament, since I am only allowed to follow said instructions after your death, which may or may not have happened. So I'll just take my fee, shall I?' The British mystery writer Wilkie Collins, author of *The Woman in White*, obviously foresaw this problem and sensibly carried his own instructions on how to check if he'd passed on around with him at all times.

It may seem a trifle over the top to us now, but the fear of waking up dead was so strong at that time that people even left instructions that they were to be decapitated, just to make sure. But, as the saying goes, if you want a job done properly do it yourself; some coffins were buried containing knives, guns or poison so the occupants might avail themselves of a quicker means of death than suffocation. But quite probably more painful, I'm thinking.

Not everyone wanted to take such drastic measures, however. There were some brains still at work after all. The 19th century was the great age of invention, so why not invent a coffin that warned if its contents were still fresh?

Some of the thinking was not so technically hot though, such as the coffin with a spring-loaded lid, or another with an escape hatch. Which are only really useful before the burial. But, as the saying goes, if at first you don't succeed, try, try again. So they did and the 'safety coffin' spread throughout Europe and the US. In Germany alone there were 30 different designs.

What all safety coffins had in common was the means by which the 'body' could let those above ground know that it was still alive. The simplest design had a string, or strings, attached to anything that might wiggle at one end and a bell at the other, such as that of Dr Taberger of Hanover. It didn't have to be a bell of course, and alternate designs used fireworks, rockets and a red flag. One particular US coffin included a ladder and an escape tube leading up from the head of the interred, just in case no one was around to help. Once they were certain the occupant was totally dead the tube would be withdrawn allowing a flap to drop and cover the face. After all, they didn't want the thing turning into a tourist attraction.

In Altmark coffin-maker Dr Adolf Gutsmuth even had himself buried in his own design for several hours partaking of beer and sausages through its feeding tube, to advertise his wares.

As each and every technological advance around the world was made, the safety coffin inventors tried to incorporate it somehow. Objects included were mechanical air pumps, electric bells, spring-driven fans and lamps inside the coffin for viewing the face. It had taken some time but they had finally caught on to the need for air as well, so the air tube became obligatory, as did, eventually, a two-way cut-off valve (because if air can get down the tube then certain gases can come up).

Being Buried Before Your Time

My own favourite from the very end of the century comes from France. The coffin included a glass panel above the head and a spring-loaded hammer to break the glass, from the outside. Yes, the outside.

From around the same time the Chamberlain to the Czar of Russia, Count Karnice-Karnicki, invented his own safety coffin after witnessing a Belgian girl almost buried alive. His idea used the rise and fall of the chest to set off a series of signals including a flag, a bell that rang for 30 minutes and a lamp, in case it was dark.

No real account seems to have been taken of those poor souls whose breathing was so shallow that it could never set off any type of device or who may have been alive but unconscious, but I suppose what you don't know can't hurt you.

The invention of the telegraph and telephone, and equally as likely the lack of sales of some of the more extreme, or stupid, safety coffins, led to a decline in their manufacture. But the fear had not gone away; it was merely the victim of progress. There are many, mostly apocryphal, stories from the early part of the 20th century of the dead being buried with a telephone or electric alarm fitted to the coffin, or inside the tomb. There are even stories of some of these phones being later found to be off the hook. I guess even the dead can get a little tired of cold callers.

If you think that science and education have made our fear go away today, then think again. In France as recently as 1983 a coffin life detector was patented, and in 1995 an Italian inventor offered a coffin that came complete with an alarm, a torch, two-way radio, oxygen tank, heartbeat sensor and cardio-stimulator.

And finally perhaps our fear continues for good reason, for in 1993 a 24-year-old South African man was pronounced dead and spent the next two days in a metal drawer in the mortuary before being released. So was there a happy ending? Not quite, his girl dumped him; there was no way she going to marry a zombie who'd come back from the dead. Even more recently, in 2003 an 80-year-old Indian man 'woke up' minutes before being hoisted onto his funeral pyre when he was splashed with the traditional cold water during the final preparations. Apparently he remarked, 'It's very cold.'

Worried? In that case, you might like to consider following the example of more and more prospective corpses and have your cell phone buried with you. In fact, such is the belief in witchcraft in South Africa that people are being buried with their mobile phones in case they aren't really dead but merely under a spell. The addition of extra phone batteries seems a little superfluous though – the air is going to run out long before the phone does.

Top ten ways to escape being buried alive

1. *It's magic:* Buy yourself a magician's coffin, maybe from the yard sale of a retired prestidigitator or from a magic shop that's going out of business. You know the type; they've a trapdoor at the back so the assistant can slip out while the illusionist pushes swords through it. There's no reason you can't simply slip out the same way, though of course this method is only useful before the interment.

2. *Deadbody.com:* Have a webcam fitted into your coffin; that way millions of surfers will be able to see your frantic wavings to alert them to your predicament. Or if you really are dead then your surviving family can make some money out of those sickos out there.

3. *That's friendship:* It's times like these when you can find out who your real friends are, so ask one to come with you. You'll need a double coffin, an oxygen cylinder for your pal when yours has run out, and another friend or two to let your friend out. And this is where they find out who their real friends are.

4. *Rumour has it:* Why not let it be known, widely, that you're going to be buried with your priceless collection of Elvis memorabilia? You'll be back up again before the dirt has had time to settle.

5. *Man's best friend:* Get a dog, or even better get more

than one. Why? Because dogs are supposed to know when their master or mistress is dead, and hence when they are alive. Then all you have to do is work out the answer to the question: if it takes one Scottish terrier 40 minutes to shift 1 square foot of earth, how many Dobermanns will it take to get down to you?

6. *Hot, hot, hot:* Perhaps the most obvious way, and let's face it it doesn't come any more obvious than the Australian advert for cremation, is to opt to be heated up. Although there's an old proverb that says something about 'out of the frying pan and into the fire'.

7. *Above us the waves:* A simple way to make sure you're not alive beneath 6 feet of mother earth is to be buried at sea beneath 600 feet of water. Ah yes, I think I see the flaw in this plan as well now.

8. *A tip:* Since the tradition is for the gravediggers to wait until the funeral party has left the area before filling in the grave – it would be kind of tactless otherwise – why not get to your loved ones to tip them to wait an extra couple of hours, until you're sure your air will have run out, before they get to work with their shovels?

9. *Rattle and roll:* If you know you're a particularly heavy sleeper why not get the pall-bearer to give the coffin one last good shake before the fateful moment?

10. *Denial:* You could always do what I intend to do and tell everyone you're simply not going.

Chapter 4
Little Boxes

It's traditional

If it was good enough for our ancestors then it's good enough for us, and today the majority still meet with those cardinal elements designed to greet death in a wooden overcoat. The traditional wooden thin – bit wider – thin again coffin is widely available; there's even a funeral super-market in the US to enable you to browse, select and push your trolley to the car park, all in one exciting shopping experience. Some funeral directors even take frequent-flyer miles. It can't be long before one of the home shopping channels has 'coffin hour', can it?

As long as you match the one-size-fits-all measurements of the standard coffin, your choice is endless. If you're especially tall or especially small, however, you'll probably have to order a bespoke model. You don't want them to have to shoehorn you in, nor do you want all that free space in which to rattle around. Then there's the width factor, and, even though in the US the width of the average coffin has grown from 21 to 24 inches, when it comes to coffins big is not necessarily beautiful. If you're having trouble dieting you might like to use the following as motivation: if you're too overweight you may need more than the usual number of pall-bearers, the gravediggers will demand overtime and since the number of crematoria equipped to handle the more ample-sized coffins is few you will force your surviving relatives and friends to travel to who knows where just to see you off. One family in the UK had to travel almost 120 miles to find one suitable for their 20-stone-plus relative. Nor do you want to have to journey to Indiana, USA, just to buy a double oversized casket or end up like one poor Cincinnati woman whose relatives had to sit on the lid to try and get it closed, and failed.

So if your taste is for the traditional (though in Italy you're pretty much restricted to the wood and tin-lined variety anyway) then simply check out the Internet and let your fingers do the walking or catch the ads on TV or radio. You'll find that some coffins even come with a life-time guarantee. As one Brazilian purveyor puts it, 'Our clients have never come back to complain.' In Wales you can even order your coffin with your Campari while you're at the bar of a certain pub. The landlord will serve you your drink, measure you up and construct the coffin for you after closing time.

The Chinese also like to be well prepared for the big day and will invite their neighbours round to admire the detail and workmanship on the beautiful coffin their loving son has provided for them.

In the US the sale of interment vessels is big, no huge, business, and though they still offer you the time-honoured oak, walnut, pine or mahogany options they'll probably point out to you that metal is the new wood. It's much trendier to have a cool brushed-steel alloy model isn't it? It'll match your kitchen appliances. Though you could really push the boat out and go for copper or bronze, if you don't mind the constant polishing.

The very latest in the traditional coffin, at least US style, seems to be aimed at those who want to hang around a while after they've gone. For some the 100 to 300 years it might take for a solid wooden coffin to become indistinguishable from its surroundings is too short, so there's the alternative concrete or reinforced fibreglass remains receptacle (and you don't get much more non-biodegradable than concrete). And, as if that wasn't enough to protect you when you're dead, some are even supplied with an inner lining constructed of the stuff they make American Football helmets out of, with a warranty that they can withstand 5,000 pounds of pressure per square inch and will not let anything in, or out, for 500 years. You could probably survive a nuclear war in one, if you weren't already dead.

And just to make sure you don't start the back-to-nature process before the main funeral event, a South African has designed a cooled coffin able to preserve bodies for up to a month.

This may all sound a trifle expensive, and it is. So what do you do if you still want a conventional coffin but don't have money to burn, or bury? Well, you might consider renting one. In Canada, and to some extent in the US, you can hire a coffin for your funeral. There's no need to worry about the possible nasty habits of the previous tenant as the rent-a-casket comes with a pine or plywood inner for your own personal use and all at a fraction of the cost of buying the whole shebang. It's not hugely popular as yet, and I'd guess that those who do use the service are going to be mostly male. No woman is going to risk her funeral guests turning to each other and saying, 'Isn't that the same coffin Maisie Clifford wore to her funeral last month?' I just can't see it happening somehow.

In the UK it is also known for some Co-operative Societies funeral departments to offer re-usable coffins, the recipient being housed in a body bag for the days and hours before the final disposition. Bag or box, it's a cheap and socially responsible idea, which brings us to the next set of alternatives.

Thinking outside the pine box

There's a growing movement among the planet-conscious corpse away from coffins with a half-life longer than the average disposable nappy to more environmentally friendly containers. It's hardly surprising more of us want a 'green' ending when it's said that loggers waste 28 trees for every mahogany example they call timber on. The Americans apparently bury or burn some 60 million feet of mainly hardwood yearly. That's a lot of trees no longer producing oxygen, which the dead no longer need, admittedly. Added to that amount of wood, they also use some 100,000 tons of steel, 3,000 tons of copper and bronze and well over 1.5 million tons of reinforced concrete per year. Oh and over 800,000 gallons of embalming fluid, since along with Canada embalming is routine in the US.

Why not choose a biodegradable coffin to complement your biodegradable body? (Well, most of most people's bodies anyway. There are gold/silver teeth, plastic hips, prosthetic limbs, glass eyes, metal pins used to secure broken bones and sundry items that have accidentally or otherwise found their way inside the human body that have to be considered. Not much you can do about the internal bionic parts but to be green you should perhaps make arrangements for the removal of all things meant to be easily detachable. And for those of you considering plastic surgery: do you really want some future Indiana Jones to excavate your remains to find that all that remains of you are two breast implants and your pair of JLo butt extensions?)

In Australia, New Zealand and Switzerland you can choose a cardboard coffin; they come flat-packed ready for assembly in five minutes apparently (although you should remember that five minutes in flat-pack time is more like an hour in normal human time). The Swiss version is said to be able to hold up to 440 pounds as opposed to the Aussie model that is only allowed to take 220 pounds by law and is for cremations only, while the Kiwi model is marketed as very good for burials at sea. It might be even cheaper to use one of those large boxes your new fridge freezer arrives in. You'll reach the end of the road advertising Zanussi, but at least your pall-bearers will be instructed 'This Way Up'.

You could consider woven bamboo, the ancient Chinese choice for coffin material and now being manufactured by them for export, though be wary of the assembly instructions. Or from a process that comes from the same part of the world you could opt for a papier mâché coffin. In Zimbabwe the rural population keep down funeral costs by using a canvas casket; it's light and easy to transport, before it's occupied obviously.

A green funeral service in London, UK and a firm in Babice, Poland offer wicker coffins. This is technically wood, but it can be harvested from the living tree and twisted into the required shape so is still an environmentally sound choice. They sell well in Great Britain, Germany and the Czech Republic, and are the 'in thing' with the celebrity set – Adam Faith, a British pop star and actor (from the time when we still called them pop stars) was buried in one.

Perhaps one of the greenest of all coffins comes from Australia and is constructed of recycled newspaper. The manufacturer stresses its strength, claiming to be able to jump up and down on a supported example, although I have no idea why you'd want to do such a thing.

The important thing to remember is not to spoil the whole ecological footprint thing by having brass handles or nameplates fitted; it kind of ruins the sentiment.

Do it yourself

Yet another fun alternative in your choice of coffin is the DIY model. Yes, it takes a little forward thinking and good timing, but why not? You don't have to be a master crafts-man; it's only a box after all. My own father had intended to use his woodworking skills to construct his own recep-tacle but a combination of lack of time and the horror on my mother's face when he announced that the only feasible place to complete such a task was on the dining room table meant that it didn't come to pass before he did. The idea was less of a problem for one London widow who happily had a friend construct her husband's coffin on the kitchen dining table. Her story also clearly illustrates one of the problems with self-build, though happily they managed to spot the box was some 6 inches too long for the grave before the actual day and modified it accordingly.

If you're not quite sure how to get started there are now plenty of books, such as *The Natural Death Handbook*, available on ecological or organic funerals containing chapters with various designs and assembly instructions to help you. After that it's all down to you; it's your design, it's your choice of material; you need only consider whether you intend burial or cremation. Some things burn better than others, after all.

One prospective occupant of a home-made coffin decided to make it double the usual width, not that he was overweight but in case he and his wife should die concurrently. Sweet, don't you think? Or he may have been thinking it was time for suttee to make its long-awaited comeback.

The other advantage of planning and putting together your own coffin in advance of its big day is that you can put it to an alternate use first if you want. In Western Europe there are examples of shelves being added to the coffin to transform it into a bookcase. No doubt containing such volumes as *Death in Venice*, *Death on the Nile*, *Death in the Afternoon*.

Coffins, home-made or not, have also found use as other items of furniture, such as an occasional table, a blanket/towel chest and even a window seat constructed by simply adding upholstery and a hinged lid. Definitely conversation pieces, don't you think? One English chap used his casket as a coffee table but may have gone a little too far when he asked the two kindly voluntary aid workers not to disturb his wife while she was in it as it was the quietest she'd been in years, after which it became a police incident.

The more Gothic among us have even been known to sleep in their coffin – I suppose it's good practice for when that sleep becomes eternal – and then there are those for whom it is yet another sex toy, but that's a different book entirely.

If having an obvious coffin hanging around, with or without shelves, isn't quite for you then a US manufacturer called Casket Furniture will happily disguise it for you as a phone booth, a home entertainment system or even kick-ass stereo hi-fi speakers.

Go your own way

There's no need to let your lack of handicraft skills prevent you from joining the increasing number of us who want more than a factory-fit sarcophagus and are looking for some individuality. We all long to be different and if it takes our death to prove we are not merely one of the pack then at least we're going to go out with a little individuality.

The simplest thing people can do to personalise their coffin is to add a dash of colour. On the west coast of the US, caskets are available in deep polished, high gloss, metallic colours that only require some wicked wheels to turn them into hot rods. Which is just what they do in Houstonville, USA when they have their annual casket race. The three-person team consists of one casket occupant and two pushers, though it might be more of an unintentional road safety infomercial than a race.

Simple highly polished white coffins add a little lightness to the proceedings and are also particularly popular in the US, as are those painted in the colours of the New York Yankees baseball team or the Oakland Raiders American football team. But only if you happen to follow those teams. The British soccer fan is similarly able to choose a red and white coffin if he supports Manchester United or Arsenal, a totally red version if he loves Liverpool and a blue and white one if he wants to tell everyone he was a Chelsea fan. The problem with this is that teams wear the same colours. In which case the name and badge of the team can be emblazoned somewhere conspicuous, such as in the lining of the coffins made in Bogota, Columbia, where they can opt for a green casket if they're Atlético Nacional till they die (which they obviously have) or a red casket if they'd die for Independiente Medellín (which they may also have done).

I suppose a logical progression from football badges, if somewhat less mass marketable, is the firm in Tennessee, US, which offer coffins sporting the logos of major universities.

But why stop there? Why not turn the whole thing into a work of art? A San Francisco firm will sell you a casket covered in pop art or graffiti, though perhaps not of the 'Steve luvs Sonya' or 'Tracey M is a bitch' variety.

If you want them to really 'Pimp My Casket', the same company offers a gold painted edition with leopard skin print interior, or you might consider a purple, green and red example with silk tassels and plastic jewelled handles. You might, but maybe not.

And the US funeral artists don't stop there. The country that gave birth to Tiger Woods can offer you a casket painted with holes from a favourite golf course, called Fairway To Heaven. Then there's their 'Great Outdoors' range where majestic eagles soar over crystal blue lakes and mist-covered mountains. For those who wish to be a little less noticeable they produce a camouflaged coffin, you just have to be careful to remember where you put it down.

Into AOR (album oriented rock to you)? Then the band KISS market their own branded coffin complete with logo and a photo of the band; it even lets you party on before or after death by including a cooling pump for the chilled beer.

And the one I have to have is painted to look like a parcel and has a 'Return To Sender' sticker slapped on it. You don't even have to be an Elvis fan either, thank you very much.

I suppose what dies in Vegas, stays in Vegas and if it does they'll sell you a casket neatly embroidered with dice and cards. And how long before someone constructs a coffin with a craps table as its lid, so your friends can have one last game on you, literally?

Even though these are not your average, everyday coffins, it's still not individual enough for some corpses. An organisation called Life Art in Australia will customise coffins for you. Life Art – in the same way Aussies call red-headed people Blue, I suppose. Customers can have the lid decorated with the occupant's name, nickname, a salutation and relevant or personal verses. Or they can supply you with a canvas coffin and coloured crayons so you can do it yourself, which is perhaps the ultimate in coffin personalisation. In England an ice cream seller had his lid covered in photographs of 99s (the ice creams with chocolate flakes stuck in).

People have found that a plain white coffin, or one of the cardboard variety previously mentioned, are ideal to let their family and friends loose on. Collages, drawings, poetry, signatures and little messages all find their way on to any available clean area. It gets treated like it was a whole body cast, though it's best to avoid 'get well soon'. The family of one home-decorated coffin in the US even dipped the paws of the family dog in mud and added his prints to the personalisation process.

And that's still not enough for some; coffins now come in all shapes and sizes, as long as there's enough room for the pilot. The fantasy coffin seems to have had its genesis in Africa, and in Ghana in particular, where several practitioners produce coffins for the dead relevant to their lives: a character trait, their profession or standing in the community. Thus rich or powerful Ghanaians have been laid to rest in a Mercedes car, a KLM airliner, a tower-shaped throne, even a mobile phone design coffin, and come to think of it that would be so perfect for my daughter. Some of the other examples need a little more explanation: the woman who was buried in a giant chicken because it represented her as the mother figure looking after her chicks or children is understandable; the fisherman buried in a fishing canoe is pretty obvious as is the leopard, the bull and the eagle, and I'll even give you the shark and the running shoe, but why the lobster, shallot, or outboard motor coffin? The opposite to such metaphorical casketry can also be found in Ghana, and is much more of the what-you-see-is-what-you-get variety: the glass coffin.

The export of the Ghanaian fantasy box to places such as Kenya, Spain and California also seems to have created a demand in the rest of the world for a little fantasy of their own. Thus in the US it's possible to make a good end in a beer bottle, or cola if you don't drink, in a steam train, a steamboat or a motor car. I guess you choose the make and model. And in the case of José Gomes, a Portuguese carpenter, that does indeed mean constructing his own coffin replica of a Mercedes 220 so when his time comes he can go in style.

The British have not been slow to take up the challenge and firms throughout the Isles will happily see you off encased in a canal boat, an energy drink can, a cricket bag and stumps, a skateboard and even a Red Arrows aerial display team jet aircraft. The friends of the environment need not feel left out either, as it is possible to buy a coffin shaped like an acorn.

If the choice is all a little too much for you then why not peel away the whole outer shell and be buried, do the ashes to ashes thing in a plain simple shroud, or follow the Jewish tradition and go on your way draped in plain white linen garments?

Taking it with you

Whatever the outer packaging, you don't have to be the only contents. We have rediscovered the possibilities of grave goods and more and more of us are taking our goodies to the grave with us. Though not so much in the UK, since a law has been passed limiting the contents of any coffin for cremation to natural substances only, so no rayon suit for the deceased for starters, which can only be a good thing. The laudable idea behind such a law is to cut down on pollution. So if you want to take it with you in Britain, get yourself buried. Which is exactly what one horse-loving Brit did, taking her saddle and bridle with her, as did the self-styled New Age wizard who was interred in his cloak, clutching his magic wand.

Some cultures never actually abandoned the idea of grave goods, such as the Algonkian peoples of Canada, who are buried with a medicine bundle, corn with a bowl and spoon and a pipe and tobacco. Tobacco and pipes also form part of the gifts to the dead in areas of the old Soviet Union, where regional variations on the grave goods theme include strong drink, combs, a handkerchief and soap and a towel. Opinion is divided from Baltic country to country as to whether to put money into the coffin – the Georgians on the whole being for it and providing a nice thick wad for your afterlife purchases, oh and some sweeties.

There was a time when the Scots would rest a plate on the chest of the deceased containing salt and earth to represent the soul and the final destination of the body. In Estonia you seem to have needed your crutches, walking sticks and glasses in the afterlife. Along with all the general items, the inhabitants of countries from Finland north and westwards were given to asking for specific items to be placed with them, a favourite ornament, a musical instrument, even a weapon. And their wishes were usually granted thanks to the belief that the dead would haunt the dreams of the living if they were not.

I've already mentioned the penchant the South Africans have for taking their mobile phones on their final journey. Well, they're not the only ones. It's pretty popular in Ireland and the US too, where they first found out about the practice when the cell phones started exploding during cremation. The inclusion in the casket is not always intentional however, as one Belgian family discovered at a funeral in Rochefort, when the corpse received a call on his mobile.

Pragmatic as ever, where the placing of the phone in the casket was likely to add unintentional fireworks to proceedings, Irish undertakers simply offered to add people's beloved phones to the ashes after the dead had been on the high heat. And though they felt no need to ban the phone from the service, they did ask that during the ceremony phones should be switched off or at least set to vibrate.

Of course cell phones are not the only items to accompany the Irish dead: other modern grave goods have included a favourite teddy bear, more than one bottle of whisky and one old boy took a packet of cigarettes and a box of matches with him.

Meanwhile back on the west coast of America, home of television and Hell's Angels, a chapter member was cremated with his switchblade knife, his brass knuckles and one final spliff, and a woman was interred with a portable television tuned to the channel running her favourite soap operas. The question is: does she count in the viewing figures?

In Australia it has become a status thing to take your more bling possessions with you, meaning that some Aussies meet their maker wearing their Armani suits, diamond jewellery and Rolex watches. One cobber even insisted on taking his cell phone, laptop and Blackberry with him.

The famous are not immune to post-mortem attachments. Tiny Tim, the high-pitched flower-power-era singer, was interred with his trademark ukulele, and Bela Lugosi, who played Count Dracula many times in the movies, wore the costume in which he had played the count, complete with cape.

All this seems pretty normal though, when compared with Russian Vladimir Villisov from Mramorskoe who plans to take his extensive collection of porn with him in a specially extended coffin, or the guy who was accompanied to the grave by his faithful companion – the one with the three holes and the life-like hair.

Top ten fantasy coffins

1. *The shark:* Okay, so it's an obvious target but wouldn't you want to see your ex-wife's lawyer buried – no wait, I haven't finished yet – buried in a shark-shaped coffin?

2. *The red pepper:* Because it's symbolic of so many things: ideal for a celebrity chef, or maybe a pretty hot woman, it could be a metaphor for the cremation process or indeed for the final destination of the deceased.

3. *The egg:* What better way to go out than exactly the same way you came in?

4. *The body-shaped wicker coffin:* Absolutely perfect for the Wiccan amongst us and, if anatomically correct, ideal to let the world know what they are going to miss.

5. *The rubbish skip:* The way we live our lives now, need I say more?

6. *Ding dong:* There's a coffin on display in the UK that's made in the shape of a 100-pound giant bell for the world champion town crier – not Quasimodo, who would have been my first guess.

7. *Skis and a sledge:* This is only of much use if Hell really does freeze over.

8. *Strike a light:* If you're one of those people who constructs models out of matchsticks then why not construct a coffin out of them? Even better, use unspent matches and save on the cremation bill.

9. *Corporate:* Another way to save your dead self a little cash is to have your coffin sponsored; if you're willing to be covered in corporate logos or take your final journey in a coffin the shape of a credit card, baked beans can or running shoe, then sign up now.

10. *Rubik's coffin:* One for the gamers of the world, a coffin with sliding coloured panels to baffle your funeral guests one last time.

Chapter 5

Final and Not So Final Resting Places

Grave concerns

It's a pity, but since we live on an ever-increasingly crowded planet, the days of Robin Hood firing an arrow into the air and asking to be buried where it fell are long gone. In fact the clamour for burial space has reached such a level that when one cemetery in Melbourne, Australia, already with a waiting list of 350, announced the availability of a new tranche of plots they had people camping out overnight to be first in line. I assume they camped out at the firm's offices – coz at the graveyard, that's just wrong.

The clamour for the eternal rental has reached such a pitch in the US that there are now online sites that allow you to buy, swap and sell cemetery plots and will e-mail you when any new availabilities are announced. Yes, I did say swap. It's sort of like: 'Wanted: single plot in country location, willing to trade inner city example including unused headstone.'

Final and Not So Final Resting Places

The good thing about bodies, at least those that have been underground for a while, is that they decompose and will eventually disappear entirely. Someone just has to test the old grave for remains using a sort of seven-foot cheese taster. The device is thrust into the depths of an ancient grave and when it is drawn out with no sign of bone or clothing then the grave can be re-used. At least at present we still have this option; it's something those who come after us may have to wait much longer to consider. Remember the American 500-year guaranteed coffin? You're going to need more than a big cheese taster to get through that. And even if we could, the human body is also taking longer to decompose anyway, and not just those of us who've been embalmed. It seems we're all full of so many chemicals and preservatives from the pre-prepared, packaged, processed food in our diet that we're taking much longer to break down into our constituent parts, or to rot, to put it bluntly. And then there's the other face/figure and recreational chemicals we pump into our bodies: it's whispered that if you were to open the vault of a dead actress or two in Hollywood you wouldn't notice much change in their smiles from the day they took possession.

The eventual lack of burial space was something our forefathers must certainly have considered in much less crowded times; they came up with the concept of the ossuary after all. The removal of a person's bones to some type of charnel house has long been a European practice, and if you die today in Germany or Spain, it's good to remember that a grave isn't yours for life, or death, you know what I mean. In Spain you only rent your hole in the wall grave for ten years, though the lease is often renewable, before your bits are removed to a communal burial site. In Germany you know when the 20-year lease is running out on your not-so-final resting place as they come round and give you a sort of parking ticket for the dead, asking you to kindly move along. I'm in no way advocating a sort of more 'Edgar Allen Poe' version of suttee here, but if after you're entombed in Germany your partner is placed in the same grave as you, then the clock is rewound and your 20 years start again. Obviously to take the maximum amount of benefit from the situation it's useful if your other half can manage to survive for, oh I don't know, say 19 years, 11 months and 20-odd days after you're gone to give you enough time to dip in under the wire.

One way round the worry of ever-approaching grave wardens is to opt for what the Germans call the 'Field of the Unknown' where you can be buried in a sort of community corner of a state graveyard with no headstone to mark your passing. Yes, it's all rather anonymous but it does save your family the worry of the upkeep of the grave and having to look for alternate accommodation for you later on. Maybe for these reasons just over a quarter of the former residents of Hamburg choose to repose among the unknown.

Final and Not So Final Resting Places

There is another little wrinkle the Germans have come up with that may well be worth filing away if you're considering dying there. You can actually apply to be buried in someone else's grave before they have ceded vacant possession. You just have to agree to be buried under their name, keeping their details on the headstone. Yours will appear nowhere on the grave. It means that if your wife was constantly calling you Michael Schumacher from the passenger seat, you could actually be him after death. See, there's even the possibility of identity fraud after your lights have gone out.

I suppose while we're on the subject of less-than-eternal rest it wouldn't hurt to mention that grave recycling hasn't always been the only reason why our bodies have been bumped from the boneyard. Back in the late 18th century and for much of the 19th century, especially when our exploration turned inward to the human body, it seems we just couldn't get enough volunteer corpses to learn more about our anatomy from, or to experiment on. Enter the grave robber, usually at dead of night, by the stuttering glow of a hand-held oil lamp, to disinter the once mortal remains of a soul not quite completely cold. Medical schools and students were willing to pay a pretty price for cadavers to call their own in order to poke, prod and plunder in the name of science.

During the French Revolution your eternal slumber was equally likely to be disturbed should you have been encased in a lead coffin as part of your last rites, since the Republicans ordered all such coffins to be melted down to provide material for bullets. The expansion of the city of Paris and its engulfing of many cemeteries also led to the relocation of some 3 million bodies into catacombs under the city in former quarries. It seems you're not safe anywhere from progress, political or geographical. Though I should think the reburial in a proper grave in Cuba of the guerrilla fighter Che Guevara after some 30 years as part of the main runway at Bolivia's International Airport was something of a relief to him.

Even some of the world's most famous and best-loved authors are not immune from being asked to vacate the premises. Sir Arthur Conan Doyle, the creator of Sherlock Holmes, was initially confined on his estate at Windlesham, Sussex, England, but was later transferred to Minstead churchyard when the family sold his former home to a hotelier.

More recently, since 1998, the Chinese have excavated over 60,000 graves in order to make way for farmland. And then there are the archaeologists. Just to make sure you future-proof yourself from these people maybe it would be a good idea to take to your grave something that will last many lifetimes and says something like – 'not to be disturbed by archaeologists'. Possibly including your lawyer's details on the flip side – because who ever heard of a law firm going out of business?

Final and Not So Final Resting Places

All this doesn't mean there aren't still choices for those who want the option of having somewhere for their family and friends to visit. The number one position for a grave site is still a graveyard, either associated with a church, or, as is the custom in much of Germany, the State. The Irish dramatist Brendan Behan said, 'I want to be buried in Kilbarrack. It's the healthiest graveyard in Ireland, being near the sea.'

In the US, family plots bought and paid for years before they are needed (hopefully) are still commonplace, as are family vaults for those who can afford them. Maybe the competition from the State is actually a good thing as it has forced the Church to be a little less choosy in who they admit into their dead club. It wasn't all that long ago that interment in consecrated ground was barred to the likes of unbaptised children, those who had committed suicide and 'lunatics' – who were thought to be possessed by the devil – or, until 1975 when the church of St Mary's in Rockville, Maryland relented, if your name was F Scott Fitzgerald and your writings were deemed undesirable. At least there's no longer the need to sneak a body of one who fell into one of those categories into a forgotten corner of a cemetery. At one time in County Tyrone, Ireland it actually made a difference which sex you were, since there was situated there a men-only burial ground. It was said that those dead chauvinists would rise up and expel any female interloper from their patch.

Eco burial

Church or State are not the only choices; there are now private graveyards, especially in the US and Canada. And you don't have to be buried in a graveyard at all; well, not in the traditional sense anyway. The new kid on the block in the burial business is the green or woodland funeral. In the UK there are getting near to 200 such burial sites within the four countries alone where people can follow the example of the author Iris Murdoch and sleep forever in the forest. The body is buried in a simple grave, often surrounded by trees and with no headstone, but merely a freshly planted sapling or shrub or basic wooden cross to mark its site. Or if you choose one of the few US natural burial sites your final resting place may be marked by a boulder; or local piece of stone to the rest of us.

Other pro-green policies of the natural burial include: the banning of any embalming; the insistence on the use of basic wooden or cardboard coffins, or no coffin at all; graves to be no more than a metre below the surface to aid the body's decomposition; and the deliberate neglecting of the local flora in order to let nature have her own way. Oh, and you can dig the grave yourself if you want. Of course, this is not something you expect to do if you've paid for a churchyard interment, but it actually happened to one family from Leeds, England who arrived at the cemetery to find the undertakers had forgotten to inform the gravediggers. Faced with the prospect of a 48-hour delay to the deposit, one of the dead man's grandsons reached for the shovels. Then there was the case of Uganda's tallest man, John Apollo Ofwono, whose grave wasn't quite prepared for his 7 feet and 10 inches and caused a delay of 45 minutes while he had an extension built.

In a recent survey, 47 per cent of Brits questioned would opt for a seedling or a shrub to mark their last stop on life's journey. That sort of figure would tend to suggest that it's not all tree-hugging New Age children of the world who want a more environmentally friendly ending. Okay, so some 250 people per year opting to actually go ahead with a green burial may not seem many, but it's a start. In fact figures also show that since the first green grave site in Carlisle opened in 1993 the eco-funeral option has grown at three times the pace that cremation progressed when it was first re-introduced to the UK.

Other parts of the world haven't yet shown quite so much enthusiasm for the idea; there is, as yet, only one woodland grave site in Belgium and that is really an offshoot from a traditional graveyard with trees and the option to allow up to three bodies to occupy the same grave.

There is a natural burial site in the Netherlands at Bergerbos, which, luckily for those Germans and Belgian death tourists who might want to go out green, is just some 6 kilometres across the border. There is a movement towards the idea in Poland, France and Italy where the idea is being spread by the Capsula Mundi organisation. And, even though green sites are opening in both New Zealand, just outside Wellington, and in Australia, there still seems to be some resistance to the idea of returning to the earth as near as possible to the way we arrived on it. We may have been unable to avoid increasing our carbon footprint in life but the green funeral gives those who wish to the opportunity to leave it creating the least amount of pollution possible. When it comes down to it, we make pretty good compost when we want to. Apparently fruit trees thrive particularly well on us.

There are at present six such eco-burial sites in the US, and they are all privately owned. Ramsey Creek Preserve is situated near Westminster, South Carolina in the tree-covered Appalachian foothills of the Blue Ridge Mountains and since it is a semi-wilderness the bodies buried there are left to return to nature surrounded by trees, waterfalls and wildlife. The wildlife you'll share your earthen home at Huntsville, Texas with, in the largest of the US sites at 81 acres, includes panthers, coyotes and golden eagles. The site in Texas makes one or two concessions to the US way of death by offering third-of-an-acre family plots and allowing for benches for families to commune with nature and the dead.

If you live in San Francisco you now have the option of a green interment on a site overlooking Golden Gate National Recreation Area; strange really, you'd have thought there'd be more facilities in the home of the hippy. On the other side of the country there are examples in upstate New York at Green Springs, Cayuga Lake and at Glendale Memorial Nature Reserve, though due to one of the local laws they cannot charge you for the burial itself but can charge for the opening and closing of the grave space. Even the Congressional Cemetery in Washington is now considering a green section, so watch this space. Or that space.

And if you're wavering, consider the motto of the Green Springs Natural Cemetery Association: 'Save a Forest – Plant Yourself'.

Home alone

Official graveyards, green or otherwise, are not a corpse's only choice. Just as the Greeks did so many years ago, the people in Ghana are sometimes known to bury their dead in the floors of their houses. I'd worry it might all get a bit *The Tell-Tale Heart* if it were my house. At least when the Amazonian Shaur peoples bury the alpha male in a hole in the floor of his house – sat on a stool for comfort – they then abandon the property to the mercies of his spirit.

The Sulawesi Islanders bury their dead halfway up a cliff face in stone-sealed holes in the rock guarded by an effigy of the dead person. And in the US it's still your right if you own rural farmland to be buried there.

In England you could consider following the example of romance novelist Barbara Cartland and be buried in your own back garden. It was also the choice of architect Friedensreich Hundertwasser who was buried in his New Zealand garden, minus coffin. Apparently in England and Wales it's easier to get permission to be buried amongst your beloved roses and rhubarb than it is to build an extension to your house. I say easier – it's not that easy, as you will have your neighbours to contend with should they object, especially if there's a covenant on your house forbidding you to do anything to adversely affect the value of neighbouring properties, and the view of a grave next door from a bedroom window might not be such a good selling point. These were the problems encountered by one widower in Dover, England. He was served with an injunction, though his wife was finally secretly interred by a group of well-meaning supporters, thus enabling him not to be the one breaking said injunction.

But house-price worries aside, it seems all you have to do to have Granny join all your other pets beneath your lawn is to make sure you tell the registrar where the grave is and check that you not within 10 metres of standing water or 50 metres of a drinking source, for obvious reasons. Then all you need to do is include it in the property deeds and perhaps plan not to move on for a while. Let's face it, decking or a water feature may add to the selling appeal of your property, but a grave? Not so much. Oh, and perverse as it may seem, the thing you might need to obtain planning permission for is the headstone.

And the sea shall have them

Burial at sea has long been a favoured means of body disposal with sailors over the centuries. You can easily understand why in the days of voyages that might last months, the need not to store the dead until home was regained was more than the simple exigencies of sailors' superstitions. Yes, the smell might have become a bit much.

So the corpse was normally wrapped in a winding sheet of sailcloth, weighted down with cannon shot and offered to Poseidon. Today, now that the time at sea need only be measured in hours from the nearest port, burial at sea has become a choice, rather than a necessity. The draw is so strong, however, that those nations with navies and a sea-faring tradition still regard it as the last right of the seaman, sailor or fisherman to rest beneath the waves. The Church of England has even added a special wording for services at sea in the *Book of Common Prayer*.

Of course in most sea-swept countries you don't have to be nautical to be interred among the fishes; there was a time when a water burial was the favoured method of body disposal of the Mafia apparently. In the US, however, it is normally reserved for those who are active, retired or honourably discharged veterans of the US military, or at least related to one of them. If your American loved one chooses to go this way you won't actually get to see it as the service takes place during naval manoeuvres. You will be sent photos or a video, though. The law didn't deter a Californian woman in her desire to descend to the depths in a hand-carved canoe. Legal or not, she was shipped out on a rented fishing boat some 15 miles and allowed to gently slide under. It's a big ocean and I guess the authorities aren't going to waste time and money looking for one tiny little canoe.

The British are less strict about the 'whom', but a little more rigid about the 'where'; they have a designated burial plot in a given part of the ocean. It's up to you how you get there and some fishermen will supplement their income by ferrying out one or two of the estimated 50 bodies each year who opt for this form of funeral. Since one of the burial grounds is some 8 miles off Newhaven in Sussex and requires a five-hour round trip, the actual funeral service is sometimes held quayside for those who worry about a little mal de mer.

Not everyone is a fan of burial at sea. The coroner of the Isle of Wight gets to see the results when the bodies that haven't been weighed down enough wash up on shore. And it's not the sort of thing you'd take home from the seaside as a souvenir.

The journey to the burial site off the coast of Merimbula, Australia must take even longer since it is 40 kilometres out to sea, after which there's the 2,000-metre drop to the ocean floor – no waiting for the thud then.

And, okay, it's not strictly salt water, but if you wish, and it's your religion, you can be floated away down the River Ganges. Quite peaceful, I would have thought.

The how

You might well be thinking that, whether churchyard, graveyard or wilderness, the actual form of burial itself is pretty much a given – you're boxed or unwrapped and laid out horizontally in a coffin-shaped hole, six feet deep. Well, not necessarily.

The first thing to consider is direction. Religion still has a huge say in the way we face when we are buried. In general, our graves are dug so that we are left facing the direction of our particular eternity or Heaven. So the Muslim points towards Mecca, most Native American tribes will face west, as do the Fijians and Samoans, and my wife, if she ever goes, will face Selfridges.

Then there's pitch and yaw, though when it comes to graves there's much less yawing than there is pitching. Many eastern countries make use of the perpendicular burial, though there are examples in the west too. The English playwright Ben Johnson is thus buried in West-minster Abbey in London. No such grand religious gesture appealed to John Baskerville, designer of the Baskerville typeface. He was originally a letter cutter on gravestones and gave his name to the building in Birmingham where I found my first student employment as a tea lady. Basker-ville was an atheist and asked his wife to have him buried perpendicularly in their garden, which she dutifully did.

If we continue the pitch one way we find that once again the overcrowding of our planet plays a part and has led to the recent decision to offer burial standing up. A cemetery outside Melbourne, Australia offers just that option. It seems you're buried 10 feet deep facing the beautiful Mount Ele-phant. I guess 10 feet to avoid the possible embarrassment of a Uganda's-tallest-man situation, this time with a head sticking out. The Malaysians and New Zealanders are also considering offering their dead the vertical choice.

Pitching a little further will eventually turn us upside down, the option for the family who want their dead to face the way they think they are bound or, according to other superstitions, to prevent them returning to haunt the living. Or you could just be nutty, as in the case of the English eccentric Richard Hull who was buried beneath a tower on Leith Hill, not only upside down but mounted on horseback.

Making your mark

The world consists of two kinds of people. There are those who are happy to return to whence they came with the minimum of fuss and who are happy to leave little, if any, trace of themselves behind. (You know, the type of person who wants to be buried under an ancient oak tree with an acorn for a headstone, and might have always worn sandals in life.) Then there's the other kind of person, who wants his or her exit marked by something, anything, no matter if our memory of them only lasts as long as we do and whose names will one day become either curiosities for those walking through graveyards years hence, or gold dust for those searching headstones for holes in their family trees. The world it seems at present is still mostly filled with the latter variety.

Okay, so we aren't all Pharaohs, we can't all have pyramids built that take 20 years are 450 feet high and cover 14 acres – not even the George Clooneys or Brad Pitts of this world quite merit that anymore – but we can still opt for the ever-popular vault. The vault, a little house for the dead to live in, though mostly out of fashion in Europe, is still a top seller in the US. You've all seen them; they come in various shapes and sizes, from simple rectangular boxes to ornate mini Colosseums, gothic temples or Ionic pillared edifices. The one thing they have in common, apart from the stiff inside, is that they all scream out 'remember me!' The Jamaican reggae star Bob Marley is confined in one such huge mausoleum behind his birth house in Nine Miles, Jamaica.

Vault central in the US is New Orleans, and if you've seen *Easy Rider* you'll know what I'm talking about – assuming you weren't merely watching the doped-up sex scene that is. New Orleans at least has an excuse for so many above-ground burials; the city sits below the water table. The reason why the rest of the country finds such monolithic structures so desirable is less clear, thought it shows no signs of ending the love affair. It is now even possible to buy yourself a composite, easily transportable, fibreglass vault. Apparently it has a butyl seal for permanent protection and can stand up to 1,500 pounds of pressure. It would probably make a great shed if you bought one ahead of the event too.

Final and Not So Final Resting Places

These days the rest of Europe tends to reserve the vault for its famous, or its loved, or both. Lenin lies in a vault, though because of its size it's really a mausoleum, as does Princess Diana of the UK. It's an option, but a pretty expensive one, and possibly says a lot more about you than perhaps you want it to, but that's just my opinion. A little journey to Samegrelo, Georgia, will show us that you don't actually have to be that famous to make a funeral fuss, since some of the tombs there can be the size and shape of two-storey houses and are filled with the owners' former possessions, from motor bikes to their entire wardrobe to a fully stocked bar. And it can be all illuminated by a myriad of twinkling lights.

The alternative to the vault or mausoleum is the crypt, either over or under ground, and it is a favourite among the Latin countries of the world, whether it's the single occupancy model or the sub-let option. The latter is mostly the method of choice; coffins are sealed side by side in loculi and stacked like a giant IKEA warehouse up to two storeys high. In Sao Paulo, Brazil and Genoa, Italy there are even crypts ten storeys high. It makes you sort of wonder whether God has to give his angels a shopping list and one of those tiny pencils, doesn't it? 'I'll have aisle four, shelves D, E and P, and aisle 27 rack A to L, oh and one of those wavy mirror things.'

Those of us with boundary issues can still find ourselves a nice little grave somewhere if we look hard enough and then take our pick from the multiple-choice of modern grave markers. We were not always so blessed; there was a time when the choice was simply this stone or that stone, depending no doubt on which one your family could actually lift. Now we are presented with a cornucopia of choice, from the archaic images of death and decay – skulls, rotting flesh and winged demons, to the simple name, rank and number, accompanied by a basic border of stones, beloved of the Germans.

And in between? Well, there's the ornate funeral art of the Italians, angels, cherubs and full-scale effigies of the deceased in some sort of heroic pose, the rider on his horse of the Georgians of Samegrelo or the Japanese gravestone that is a complete marble set of coffee table and 'comfy' chairs that allow the living to sit and chat with the interred one.

Gravestones weren't originally made to mark graves. The idea was that by sealing the grave with a huge boulder it stopped the spirit climbing back out again. The concept of marking the grave in order to keep in some sort of touch with the dead may well have come to the fore around the same time we finally figured out that just because people were dead it didn't necessarily mean they'd got the hump with the living.

Final and Not So Final Resting Places

For those in need of the personal touch, there's always the lifelike bust, such as that of Jim Morrison, the lead singer of The Doors, in Paris, or that of Karl Marx, the lead singer of communism, in Highgate Cemetery, London. There are always some for whom a bust is never enough, and the grave of the Irish writer and wit Oscar Wilde is an anatomically correct Egyptian male figure sculpted by Jacob Epstein. Or at least it *was* anatomically correct. It seems the local mayor decided that the statue shouldn't be quite so in your face and ordered a fig leaf to cover the offending anatomical correctness. And when there was a more enlightened attempted to remove the fig leaf in protest at censorship the figure was left even less correct.

For those wanting something a little more this millennium then there's the mobile phone-shaped grave cover, no doubt with God on speed dial. But if you really want to get down with grave fashion you really have to check out what's on offer in the US. Here they have glow-in-the-dark headstones, and not just for Halloween. You don't have to conform to the traditional-shaped gravestone either, as examples also now come in the circular ying-and-yang motif for the spiritual or in the form of Bart Simpson or Eeyore for the ... less spiritual. And if you really want to have the last word you can even video an ultimate message to those you leave behind and have it played in a continuous loop on a solar-powered, weatherproof, seven-inch LCD screen set in your headstone.

Give it a couple of years and headstone technology will catch up with home entertainment technology and you'll be able to pre-program a holographic version of your head with a certain number of set phrases in order for your surviving relatives to be able to have an actual conversation with you when they visit. Trust me, it's coming.

If this all sounds a little too *Star Trek* for you then maybe you should think a tad more retro and go for the personal touch. The turn of the 19th century saw some US families have their children's favourite toy enclosed in glass and displayed with the child's remains. Or why not be your own headstone? There was a time in when it was considered cool to remove the head of the decedent and display it in a small church-shaped box. Thinking about a nice cool slice of marble with 'Rest in peace' on it? Me too.

Top ten fantasy headstones

1. *Chicken exit:* How about one of those signs you sometimes see as you're queuing for a scary ride at a theme park that tell you 'there's still time to turn back'? Or maybe the one that tells you that 'the wait is eternity from this point'?

2. *Good boy:* You could always wind up a few passers-by with one of those terrible tacky garden ornament things

that consists of the rear half of a dog apparently disappearing into the ground.

3. *Smile:* Or, even better, why not have a totally lifelike sculpture made of just your head to use as a gravestone?

4. *McGrave:* If fast food was your life, or possibly your death, why not rest beneath a set of golden arches?

5. *What a dish!:* Have a satellite dish as your headstone. Why not, they're popping up everywhere else?

6. *Convenient:* Not that I'm in any way endorsing the idea, but for the widow who's been cheated on there's always the headstone in the shape of a public urinal for the dead husband.

7. *Naughty:* Why not do like those who once lived in the Far East once did and have erotic scenes on your tomb or headstone? Obviously the grave would have to be in a curtained off area of the graveyard with a strict over-18 visiting rule.

8. *Me and my car:* You can have your very own miniature Cadillac Ranch if you bury the front half of your car, leaving the rest above ground as your headstone.

9. *Crochet:* Why not knit your own headstone ladies, or gents – let's not be sexist.

10. *It's alive:* There are enough out-of-work actors and drama students making a living as human statues, so you could probably convince one to be a living headstone, at least for a while.

Chapter 6

Light My Fire: Cremation

Over the last 130 years cremation, or simply put – setting fire to the body – has made something of a come-back in the Western world. Perversely, for a Catholic country (Catholics normally reserved the flames for heretics), the first public crematorium was opened in Milan, Italy in 1876. I guess it was some sort of throw-back to the Ancient Roman funeral pyre. And, of course, the funeral pyre itself had never actually gone away, it is still the choice of the world's Hindus as their preferred mode of final disposition.

For those Hindus who have travelled far from the River Ganges and cannot afford to have their ashes returned to its banks to be cast upon her surface, it is now possible to import her waters. When the ashes are to be scattered they are mixed with the bottled liquid of mother Ganges and scattered over a local canal, river or stream. One firm from Barrow upon Soar, England takes parties out on a canal boat for just such a service. The other alternative is to actually have the stretch of water concerned declared part of the Ganges by means of adding a little of the original and blessing it.

There are also now crematoria in Britain that will cater for that other Hindu tradition of the eldest surviving son lighting the funeral pyre of his parent by providing a button for him to press, in private, that will fire up the furnace.

In England the renaissance of the cremation all started with a Druid, Dr William Price, who was arrested trying to burn the body of his dead five-month old son on a hillside, but won his case in court and the cremation went ahead. You have to admire his part in the movement towards cremation, and the fact that he sired a son at 83. That particular legal loophole appears to have been closed today, however; a man from Leeds wound up in court for not telling anyone his mother had died and cremating her in her rear garden. But then maybe he was in court because he continued not to inform anyone of her death for two years yet still somehow managed to draw her pension.

Perhaps because it is a small island with increasing pressure on graveyard space, Great Britain leads the way in Europe in choosing cremation – those facing the flames now account for almost three quarters of all disposals. The lack of space on an island, and a long Buddhist tradition are perhaps the reasons why the Japanese out-burn the British with 98 per cent of the dead population choosing cremation. Though nowhere near approaching those sorts of figures, fans of the fire in the US and Canada have risen to just over a quarter of those moving on, though the figure for California is closer to 50 per cent, and there is an interesting anomaly in the British Columbia region of Canada where that number reaches towards some three quarters. At the other end of the spectrum, cremation is practically the norm in Scandinavia, especially in those areas in the permafrost regions, the exception being Finland. I know not why, you'll just have to ask a Finn.

The French choose cremation once in every nine times, and, due to what some see as the high cost of dying, in Germany feeding the flames is now becoming an increasingly popular option, even with the extra layer of rules they have grafted on to the process compared with most of the rest of world, the rest of the world except Austria that is. The Austrians would appear to agree with the Germans that if you want to take your loved one's cremains home with you, you may as well forget it. And where you have managed to obtain the necessary permission to scatter them over one of the few designated graveyards, or if you want to spread them at sea beyond the three-mile limit, then you're not allowed to drive them there yourself. Kind of takes all the fun out of it really, and it means you can't set a road movie about travelling somewhere to scatter Nana's ashes in Germany. Unless it's a movie about an illegal journey ...

Light My Fire: Cremation

If you do decide to do the dust-to-dust thing it might be worth keeping in mind the following: it takes around 200 pounds of gas to produce temperatures of 800 to 1,000 degrees Celsius for up to four hours to turn one person into around 4–9 pounds of ash. That's even hotter than a fast-food apple pie. All of which translates, apparently, to the fact that if you live in the US you're using the power needed to drive up to 4,000 miles per person, or, if you add up all the energy in US crematoria use, the energy needed would let you travel to the moon and back over 80 times. So don't die – re-launch the space programme!

The process of turning a water-based being into a carbon-based heap also releases mercury, dioxin, hydrochloric acid, hydrofluoric acid, sulphur dioxide and carbon dioxide into the atmosphere. Some people, I'm guessing science nerds, have been known to have their pockets stuffed with certain combustible chemicals so that everyone will know that it was their turn in the flames due to the change in the colour of the smoke drifting wistfully up from the crematorium chimney. Actually it's pretty cool, though I am in no way endorsing it, much. And similarly I could in no way condone those hippies who went their way padded out with best Acapulco Gold or Maui Wowie to chill out the world, man. I mean, what a waste.

And, you know what, there's no guarantee you'll actually make it from the funeral to the flames – well, not if you were due to be reheated by a firm in Georgia, USA, run by a former college football star who inherited the family business. It seems that when the furnace gave up the ghost, so to speak, he couldn't afford to have it repaired and simply dumped his customers locally, though fairly discreetly, for the next 15 years. Obviously he wasn't too discreet as he was finally caught. At the last count the authorities had recovered over 300 bodies, or bits thereof. He got 12 years for theft, since there was no Georgia law against body dumping, and some 23 states now have pretty solid rules on cremation.

Of course if this worries you in any way you don't actually have to take the crematorium route home; if you want to witness the process yourself then open-air funeral pyres are still practised in the Eastern world and in England you can legally light up your relatives, as long as they are dead, on land you own, such as your garden, or land you have permission to use. You just need to take the usual precautions: have emergency water standing by, don't light the fire too close to flammable structures, such as wooden fences, and don't let the kids toast marshmallows on the fire – unless it was actually Granny's last wish.

Ashes to ashes

Okay, so you've been warmed through to about 900 degrees Celsius. You've been placed in a rotating chamber and had ball bearings, or steel balls, added to you and been spun to crush the remaining bony matter. You've had the ball bearings removed with a magnet and you're now simply four litres of ash; well, what are you going to do next?

The simplest answer is to actually do nothing; you've earned your rest so why not spend the remainder of eternity in an urn? The only choice you, or your family, have to make is just where the urn will find its own final resting place.

There are columbaria the world over happy and willing to receive you and display you on shelves, behind glass or totally encased. You'll be with friends and neighbours and people you've never met in your life before, so why not take the opportunity to make new friends? Being interred in a columbarium means that those you leave behind will have somewhere to visit, and maybe talk to you or bring flowers to you. All of which are said to help in the grieving process.

But what if the family doesn't want to let go just yet, or doesn't want to leave their loved one somewhere they might consider a little impersonal, no matter how well intentioned, or what if the decedent simply didn't like crowds? The thing to do is to take hubby, missus or granny home with you, making sure you don't leave her on the bus when you get off. (Yes, it was an Englishman who actually did this. I'd like to wager that there isn't a lost property office in the western world that hasn't now, or at some time had, a shiny urn full of cremains on their shelves waiting to be claimed. And I do hope they were, or are, claimed; a shelf in lost property is not somewhere to spend eternity.)

There is a growing tendency in the West to house the cremated remains of our loved ones in the home, on a shelf, above a fireplace (they're used to the heat) or maybe as a bookend amongst their beloved volumes. There seem to be no limits to the nooks and crannies the dead now find themselves resting in: former motor mechanics can be found back among their tools in the garage; cooks becomes the centrepiece on the dining tables they would use for dinner parties; I've even been told of a woman who has the ashes of her cheating husband on a shelf by her toilet, waiting for the moment she feels is right to flush him away. (Note here, boys and girls: don't try this at home since in most countries it's illegal.)

There are two places about the house that are, but should never be, the new home of the 4–9 pounds of our loved one: the kitchen, for obvious hygiene reasons, and the bedroom, for so many reasons.

Urns, but not as we know them

There are many funeral directors who will be more than willing to supply you with an average marble, alabaster, copper, or bronze urn, in the standard urn shape for you to love and cherish. Of course standard means different things to different peoples: in Italy it means classical die-cast bronzes; in the USA it can mean pewter or titanium in the shape of an angel and readily available from your local urn depot. The UK can now probably add wooden and clay urns to what are considered standard. But some people these days want a little more than that. They want something a touch more individual; something that stands out from the crowd of other urns and says something about the person contained inside. Even if that something it is saying is that the guy inside is as big a loser in death as he was in life.

Just as there are those who offer decorated coffins, there are suppliers who offer decorated urns. If you are a patriot, or jingoist depending on your point of view, then have your national flag embossed on your container. Or if you're a fisherman, the trout model is for you. Or maybe you'll hedge your bets one more time and have a prayer inscribed on the lid of your afterlife receptacle.

And just as with those who want something more than a little extra colour from their coffins, there are the urn individualisers. The greener souls are now being interred in biodegradable acorn-shaped urns, though since they are meant to break down these are probably more for the person who wants their ashes buried beneath an 800-year-old tree somewhere overlooking frolicking lambs, rather than for those who wish spend from now until doomsday on a shelf next to the china figurine they left to their daughter. There's a green sentiment somewhere in the idea behind splashing your cash on an urn for your ash that is shaped like an eagle or a dolphin, or even a hollow memorial rock, I think. Maybe; well, perhaps there is in the US, where they are produced.

At least there's an honest kitsch declaration by those who buy urns in the form of the Eiffel Tower, or in the shape of multicoloured, 17-inch tall teddy bears, and even in the group of three figures that is called the 'Family Hug'. And you have to admit there's something almost poetic in having your ash placed in a giant cigar-shaped reliquary.

Those who want to make a real display of themselves can do so, in the US anyway, by placing their ashes in the horn of a chrome rhino's head. You might think this is a little Freudian, and I'm right with you. And the same goes for the bronze urn cast from the mould of a dinosaur tooth. Staying in the States, a firm in Milwaukee, Wisconsin can supply you with what they call the Rider's Last Rest, a 250-cubic-inch urn made out of a genuine motorcycle cylinder. And if you can't bear to be parted from your loved one, they're working on a two-stroke model. Yet another company can see the late biker ensconced in the similarly named 'Born to Ride', an urn made from a converted motorcycle petrol tank and sprayed into a metallic paint work of art. Which you could actually say is a fair description of many of the urns now on offer. Of course if you're the sociable type and crave company you can purchase a tall marble reliquary that will hold the entire family.

I suppose even the blatant imagery of the parts of a motorcycle are too subtle for some since they choose a more literal-shaped ash chamber: one that represents their former occupation maybe. In the US you can choose from urns that take the shape of a firefighter, a nurse, a police officer, an American football player and – my two favourites – a teacher (though how they are meant to represent that profession I'm not sure – an ink-stained jacket?) and a 'pretty girl' (honestly!). If even that isn't quite in your face enough, why not use your own face and have a bronze likeness bust cast? Though beware: someone is bound to say that there's more between your ears now you've gone than there ever was before.

If we leave the shining shores of the US for a moment we'll see that you need not feel left out if you want something from the à la carte urn menu. In New Zealand, for example, you can be interred in an ostrich egg, while a

German firm was offering football-shaped urns to celebrate the hosting of the 2006 World Cup.

And, yes, you can buy a 3-foot high robot urn for your remains, but you don't have to buy anything at all if you don't wish to: almost anything that provides a sealable compartment large enough to fit you in can be pressed into service, and is. The cremains of one US citizen are kept in a converted liquor cabinet; it even plays 'How Dry I Am' when opened. And a columbarium in California has such varied examples of ash containers as tobacco humidors, cameras, cookie jars and coffee tins. If it's even vaguely hollow, or can be made hollow, then it can contain dead people: a picture frame, a violin, a snare drum, a guitar, a fishing rod or a walking stick. And for those who always had their noses in a book, well, why not have the rest of their selves join that nose and be sealed inside a favourite volume?

You can always put yourself to some use after you've gone, like the cremated guy who was interred into a working clock, just in case we hadn't spotted that the Rolling Stones were wrong and time is not on our side. Or the woman in England who had some of her husband's ashes sealed in a blown glass egg timer so that he'd finally be of some use in the kitchen. There's even a company who will create glass tree ornaments that contain your ashes so that you'll still be able to share Christmas with those you left behind.

And one final way of not spending money on a personalised urn is to eschew the proffered pottery option and
have one of your children, or grandchildren, make you a
clay version in art class at school. No kids? Then join an
evening class and make one yourself. It may lean a little
to one side and the glaze may have run on the 'M' so
that 'R I P Me' now reads something totally different and
hopefully untrue, but it'll be one of a kind, which really
is the way the funeral world is heading.

Scatter the matter

The cheapest urn is the one you don't have to buy, make
or convert at all, but merely borrow until your ashes are
scattered permanently to the welcoming winds. Most
undertakers provide this service nowadays.

The majority of crematoria and most cemeteries provide
a garden of rest, set aside especially for the scattering of ashes.
There's usually someone on hand to not only direct you to
that day's nominated spot (they can't have everyone's grey
matter piled up in one place now can they?) and to help
you with the dispersal. In England such places use a kind of
huge icing sugar sifter for the task; a button is pressed and
the receptacle swings gently from side to side, rather like
putting that final dusting on the cake of a person's life.

And In The End

You don't have to be mingled with others at an official site, however. If you're not planning on moving house in the near future then your own garden is a popular choice. The back-to-nature theme in general has seen an upsurge in growth in recent years, with more and more cremains being returned to the wild, in fact so much so that on Ben Nevis, the UK's tallest mountain, the amount of ash scattered there has changed the pH level of the soil and there are real worries about the environmental impact it is having. It's kind of ironic really, when you think about it. The Mountaineering Council of Scotland is urging those who wish to scatter on their peaks to do so on rocky outcrops or to bury the urn instead in order to lessen the effects.

And just as you can be buried at sea, you can also have your ashes scattered at sea, and probably with less of a voyage involved. Such expeditions venture out from the shores of Great Britain, from the South Street Sea Port in New York and even from the volcanic sands of Hawaii in a canoe. Those who begin their final voyage in New York pass both the Statue of Liberty and Ellis Island to the sounds of a violinist and oboe player from the Julliard School of Music.

For footballing landlubbers many of the British football clubs now allow the scattering of their fans' ashes in the stadium, though not so much pitch-side any more, due to the possible combination of a centre half with an open wound, a sliding tackle that takes him out of play and the cremains of old Joe, the club's number one fan. Manchester United offer a scattering service, and book for up to four ceremonies per week.

Choosing to be scattered at some other places of significance to the decedent can prove slightly more problematic. An English family managed to successfully negotiate a scattering in a pond their father loved to play in as a child that was now on private land, but the idea of one child that they scatter his gran's remains in her local Marks & Spencer's store, as it was the place she loved best, was not really on. The little chap even seems to have considered that the shop might well object and was ready with a suggestion that they empty her surreptitiously out of their trouser legs just like he'd seen on *The Great Escape*.

The urge to be different is no less evident in the dispersal of ashes than it is in the funeral as a whole. It starts with perhaps the addition of some glitter to the cremains for a sparkly spreading, then moves on to releasing them at the nadir of a bungee jump and rises to the pinnacle of being cast from the shrouds of a hot air balloon. Though if the thought of actually having to go up there to do the deed gives you the willies, then a US company in Florida can offer you the alternative of an unmanned biodegradable balloon, which bursts when it reaches roughly 30,000 feet, releasing the cremated soul into the atmosphere over Washington, Michigan, Florida or New Jersey. Sir Charles

Irving and his twin sister Libby were dropped over the town of Cheltenham in England, though I'm unsure if it was in tribute or otherwise.

Scot Jim McTaggert, a former stunt pilot and crop duster, has developed a compressed air system for firing the ashes out of the back of his 1930s-style biplane, thus avoiding the possibly of the air draft depositing your relative back in the cockpit with you or dusting up your goggles. He's also developed a system that mixes oil with the ash to produce smoke as it exits. Happy trails.

Not quite so high up but equally, if not more, explosive, is the story of an English peer of the realm who wanted his ashes blasted across his acres by an 18th-century cannon. Though they couldn't quite match the swagger of going out with such a bang, both the art historian Roger Palmer and the gonzo journalist Hunter S Thompson went ballistic when carried in specially adapted fireworks; Palmer during a bonfire party and Thompson from a 153-foot tall memorial tower. Both, no doubt, to the sound of the requisite oohs and aahs. But you don't have to be famous to be shot into the night sky; a grandmother from England also had her ashes spread over the Malvern Hills by firework. In fact it's becoming so popular in the UK that several firms have added the ceremony as one of their funeral options.

'All in one go' is not the only choice happy scatterers have; there is now also a trend to divide up the ashes of a loved one and instead of casting them to the wind, casting them to the four winds. One firm will incorporate human cremains into the soil at the base of a bonsai tree and you can purchase several if you wish so that the whole family can have a little of Grandpa. Apparently in California it has been known for the relatives not to wait for such a gift but to turn up with their own spoon and a pot plant. A Chicago animal-loving woman had portions of her ashes shipped to and scattered in Vermont, an area of rainforest in Puerto Rico and Goose Island in Chicago itself. The remaining remains, so to speak, were scattered at a pet cemetery in lieu of the actual burial there she originally wished.

The cremains of a former Irish champion clay pigeon shooter achieved the dual distinction of being both spread far and wide and going out with the obligatory bang when he was packed into shotgun cartridges and fired over his favourite shooting ranges around the world. In fact, for the US and Canadian hunter a firm called Canucks Sportsman's Memorial Inc will pour anyone into shotgun shells for their buddies to blast away with.

In an attempt to spread the ashes of his mother even further afield, a native of Inverness, Scotland put his well-travelled mother's ashes up for sale on eBay for a penny a pinch, the minimum bid allowed. He wasn't looking to make a profit, but wanted to distribute her as far as possible. He managed to solicit offers from as far away as New Zealand, Australia and a ranch in Tulsa, Oklahoma in the US, before his auction was pulled.

Then there are those people who just can't seem to get far enough away, like Gene Roddenberry and, more recently, James Doohan, both of *Star Trek* fame, and Timothy Leary, of other means of space travel fame. The Celestis Foundation, a company operating out of Vandenberg Air Force Base, California, will send some seven grams of you into earth orbit for a lower fee than the estimated $20 million-plus it would cost you to go if you were alive, though you do get less of a view. The cremains are enclosed in a little capsule inscribed with your name and epitaph – and yes, there have been several 'boldly go's – and launched into earth orbit where, until that orbit decays and you fall back through the atmosphere to burn up like shooting stars, you become temporary space junk. The family is invited to the launch and can take home a personalised video of the ceremony.

For a few dollars more you can also decide to be rocketed to the moon or even deep space. The ashes of the astronomer Eugene Shoemaker, discoverer of the comet Shoemaker-Levy 9, were crashed into the moon on the Lunar Prospector in 1999. Now that really is something totally individual; first man on the moon: Neil Armstrong, first dead man on the moon: Eugene Shoemaker.

Light My Fire: Cremation

And talking of burning up, which if you think about it is pretty redundant anyway, then though less spectacular, and less expensive certainly, the choice of an Isle of Wight steam train enthusiast and volunteer driver to take one final journey on the footplate of a twilight special before being added to the firebox probably meant as much to him and his family as it did to those ashtronauts.

There was a time when peoples from Africa would use the ashes of the dead as a condiment, and peoples of the Amazon would sprinkle their family members into a fermented drink. Both are a little too *Soylent Green* for me, and thankfully not really a death-style choice these days. However, it is rumoured that, though it was more likely part of one of his routines, comedian Richard Pryor asked for his ashes to be mixed with cocaine to let his friends really party. But I think I draw the line at that too.

If you're looking for other real options, then someone will always spot a gap in the market and fill it, unless the market comes to them of course. Bettye Brokl, a woman from Mississippi, USA, incorporated some of her mother's ashes into abstract paintings – at first just for her family but later, as word spread, as a business for other people (with their family members' ashes, of course, not her mother's). And a student at a London art school managed, through a plea on the local radio, to use the ashes of the mother of a bus driver to create a ceramic sculpture.

And In The End

Another artist, of a kind, Reverend Mad Jack will combine ashes with his inks to make memorial tattoos, if you want, and the creator of comic book hero Captain America was also mixed with ink to print a limited edition poster of the 'Squadron Supreme'.

In both the US and the UK, there are companies who will encapsulate ashes into glass ornaments such as paperweights, jewellery, wine glasses, plaques and vases. The latter might not be the best choice if you have kids, however; you really don't want to find yourself one day saying to little Johnny, 'You've broken Granny!'

There are companies worldwide who will incorporate cremains into jewellery – earrings, brooches, pendants and necklaces – so you can always have your loved one near. And if enclosing ash into jewellery isn't your thing, then what about becoming jewellery, or in fact a diamond? LifeGem, a US company, will extract the carbon from a person's ashes and heat and pressurise it until it becomes a raw diamond, ready to be faceted and polished. It takes about 11 weeks and apparently there's enough carbon in the average human body to create 50 to 150 such gems. You can be anything from a quarter carat up to two whole carats on your wife, husband or lover's ring, if you want.

Perhaps not quite such a flashy monument, but an ecologically sound choice is to become part of an artificial reef. Made out of concrete and containing the ashes of up to a hundred other planet-conscious people, the reefs form new habitats for sea life off the coasts of Florida and North and South Carolina. The company concerned tries to make the process as friendly as possible – after all, we are talking lumps of concrete here – by encouraging the surviving family members to imprint their hands in the reef while it is still wet, and take a rubbing of the brass plaque during the ceremony.

Perhaps my own favourite story in this category is that of Edward Headrick, the creator of the Wham-O frisbee, who had his ashes pressed into a special Frisbee all of his own, well, all him actually.

Top ten no-nos at the interment

1. *Dust to dust:* If you're invited to toss a handful of dirt into the grave, don't take a run-up.
2. *Beat it:* Unless specifically requested to in the will of the deceased, dancing on the grave is uncool. (Unless your tribe practises the ancient ritual of stamping the departed's spirit into the ground – though even then you really shouldn't be doing it to 'Get the Party Started' by Pink.)
3. *Short change:* If it's your custom to throw coins in after the coffin, it really isn't done to climb in to take change.

4. *Strapping:* Should you be honoured to be asked to take one of the straps that lowers the casket into the grave, it's best to refrain from offering such advice as, 'to me, to you, to me, up your end a bit …'

5. *The gift of life:* The interment is probably not the best time to announce that you've found his organ donor card.

6. *Out loud:* Nor is it the done thing to rub your hands together and announce to all that 'This is the best part!'

7. *Fun and games:* No matter how tempting, you should not nudge the person stood next to you towards the open grave, grab them before they fall and shout 'Saved your life!'

8. *Smokin':* For those who still smoke, a grave is not a six-by-three ashtray.

9. *It's over:* Once the interment is over, leave the reinstatement of the grave to the gravediggers; no one likes a smart-arse who offers to help.

10. *Tap tap:* Nor should you ask, as you are walking away, 'Can anyone else hear that knocking sound?'

Chapter 7

Other Ways of Disposing of the Body

Earth to earth

There are rumours that post-mortem cannibalism is not merely a thing of the past. However, as a way of disposing of the dead, I'd have to put it pretty much down there at the bottom of my list. Although it does save time and effort on the funeral supper.

Those who really want to be part of the circle of life could do worse than consider the Tibetan Sky burial. This burial consists of an undertaker, a machete and a flock of vultures. You can join the dots yourself, but if you can't: the body is butchered into easily digestible chunks, the bones are pounded to dust and mixed back in with the meat, a little barley and yak butter is added to taste, before it is all tied to a large flat rock under the lip-licking vultures. And since 80 per cent of Tibetans choose to return to the sky this way there are over a thousand sites dealing with up to 20 bodies a day. It may be a roundabout way but at least the bodies will eventually return to the earth, you just don't want to be standing underneath when it does.

Don't fancy it much? Well, one German farmer did and having no vulture handy when his friend died, decided the next best things would be his pigs. The Discovery Channel has a lot to answer for.

A perhaps neater way to re-commune with Mother Nature is to cut out the middleman and go straight for the compost option. The Compostorium is a sort of bio-friendly crematorium, where the body is autoclaved to nuke all the bad stuff we might have ingested or contracted, before being interred in what's basically a larger version of the composter you might have in your own garden. The mix of one part man meat to four parts vegetable matter takes about six months to turn into usable soil, as long as you jiggle the urn a bit every few days to make sure it mixes well.

Apparently the whole process is mourner and decedent friendly, as the vegetable matter can be constituted of items of choice of the passed or the living; thus you get to toss in the funeral flowers, the remains of the funeral feast or the cuttings from the deceased's pride and joy lawn, along with items of their natural fibre wardrobe or even soil from their partner who was disposed of in the same way. Just think, you can, in a very real way, be part of the prize-winning team behind your geraniums at the local flower show, years after your death. And should you choose to be scattered on your own garden, and the family some time later decides to sell up, well, there won't be that potentially awkward conversation about one particular corner of the garden there might have been.

The Swedes of Jönköping have added some high technology to the composting process for those Scandinavians who want the more personalised compost. Susanne Wiigh-Masak, a Swedish biologist who studied at Gothenburg University, uses the freeze-dry method to start the whole process off. The body is frozen to -18 degrees Celsius before it is dipped in liquid nitrogen and we've all seen the effect that has in science fiction movies – the body becomes extremely brittle and bits break off, usually the extremities first. The body is then further reduced to a fine powder by vibrating it. A vacuum chamber evaporates the water and a metal separator removes any non-organic bits accumulated over the years. The human dust is buried in a cornstarch coffin and six to 12 months later all you need to remember is where you buried it.

In the name of science

Many more of us are now choosing to take our last exit not quite as complete as when we made our entrance, ticking to become organ donors after our demise. In the US it really is a simple as ticking a box on your driver's licence application. Is this because they know that victims of car crashes are more likely to have viable organs to donate than those who die of diseases, or the fact that the victims and hence the organs are statistically going to be younger? I do wonder if those who tick the 'skin donation' box actually know that they might end up making the end of some guy's penis thicker when their purified epidermis is injected into it during what is called a dermal matrix graft.

Man's greatest gift to another man aside, there are some people who are willing to go the extra final mile and donate their entire bodies to medicine or science in lieu of burial or cremation. The obvious choice for most is to will themselves to a medical school or hospital. The English philosopher Jeremy Bentham left his body to University College Hospital, London, where he can still be seen, in period costume, today. Unfortunately, the intention of Sir Victor Horsley to leave his skull and brain to the Neurological Society in the same city rather floundered with his death far, far away in Mesopotamia.

Those who leave their cadavers to hospitals can expect to be used for instruction in anatomy, osteopathy and for practice in dissection. You may even find yourself hanging from a hook in a teaching room as a skeleton, though this is less likely nowadays. All US medical schools rely on a constant stream of donations for their students to practise on, though other countries have rather more in the way of recruitment problems. In Ghana the medical schools had to issue a plea for corpses due to the lack of suitable volunteers turning up.

If you're considering leaving your remains to a bunch of spotty med students it might be worth considering asking the institution in question just what you could be used for, and how. Did you remember to ask if your head might be removed and used during face-lift refresher courses? Because, and I'm trying to be tactful here, you might not actually find your way onto a hospital table in one piece. There are universities who slice and dice your gift and scatter it to as many departments as possible to make maximum use of you. You might even find yourself being the centrepiece of a teaching seminar, well, your knees or shoulders might. To some that's an honour, to others it's just gross.

It's also worth checking what happens when there's no more they can do with you. In the US, this normally means a brief service followed by cremation. Or if they can't use you before your sell-by date, it is just possible you might get sold on elsewhere, which in the US may well involve a body broker. If you also tick the 'can be used for medical research' box, it may just be worth checking out exactly what that research might be. If it doesn't bother you, fine, but you might want to consider a 'not to be used for' clause in your donation details if you'd rather not end up being

used, say, as a human crash-test dummy for impact toler-
ance tests. It was once one of the options on offer for the
dead at Wayne State University in Detroit, USA who had
been conducting motor safety tests since 1939, and at the
Technical University of Graz, Austria.

Of course experiments on human cadavers are not a
new phenomenon; as early as the 1700s the French used
corpses to test out the efficiency of the guillotine and later
employed one Dr Jean Baptiste Vincent Laborde to exam-
ine the severed heads of several of its victims to test the
theory that such heads remained conscious for a time after
the event. But if he didn't find any truth in the story, then
a physician called Beaurieux claims to have witnessed the
eyelids and lips moving and in one case he called out the
victim's name and the eyes opened and looked at him.

Staying with the French, in the 1930s Dr Pierre Barbet
nailed an unclaimed corpse to a cross in his Paris laboratory
in order to test the authenticity of the blood patterns on the
Turin Shroud. But it seems the dead weight proved a little
too awkward to handle and he later confined himself to
hammering disembodied arms to the cross to determine the
optimum point to nail a human wrist during crucifixion.

The Germans, the French and the Americans have all
at one time tested weapons or armour on human remains.
In the US at the Armed Forces Institute of Pathology you
might find yourself wearing a shroud of body armour being

tested, or at the US Army Ordnance Department you may well swing from a beam on a firing range while a new rifle is tested on you. All these choices and more can be yours should you leave your body to science.

It is possible to have it both ways, however, as was the case of an American widow who had the rest of her husband's ashes returned to her to put on her bedroom dresser after his head had been used for crash-helmet testing.

If you're a fan of the TV programme *CSI* (the original set in Las Vegas, of course, the other two shows in the franchise are good but you simply can't beat a bit of Grissom), then why not consider donating yourself to the Body Farm – or, less colloquially, to the University of Tennessee Forensic Anthropology Facility at Knoxville. Operating since 1971, the farm will use your remains to study body decomposition rates; you might be buried in a shallow grave, left out in the blazing summer Tennessee sun, locked in the boot of a car or even weighed down underwater. Your body may even be dressed in various clothes to discover the difference they might have on your back-to-earth regime or you may have bullets inserted into you to test the effect you are having on them as you break down. Even the soil underneath you and the bugs that take up residence inside you are tracked. And even after all that's left of you are bones, these are entered into a collection of skeletons representing the various body types – and all in the name of catching the bad guy.

The bad guy isn't always necessarily human, however. It might be, let's see, a lion. In Tanzania a villager spiked the uneaten remains of his wife in order to poison the lion that had killed her when it came back for seconds. Okay, this wasn't strictly a donation for medical purposes, but then neither, technically, is it when people give their dead selves to German doctor Gunther Von Hagens. Von Hagens uses a process called plastination, which replaces the water in the human body with polymers to prevent decay. He exhibited some 200 plastinated bodies, minus their skin and fat, initially in a converted Berlin train station but afterwards on tour throughout the world, taking in Vienna, Brussels and Tokyo, with plans to hit the US. And it seems people like the idea of 15 minutes of skinless fame since five people a day sign up for the process at each exhibition.

If you want your fame to spread a little wider then you might volunteer for one of the doctor's televised autopsies or dissections. If you'd died in 2004 you could have joined the cast of a British theatre group who were looking for a corpse for their production of *Dead … You Will Be*. And you wouldn't have had to worry about learning your lines either.

So should you wish neither the box or the flame you can be shot at, crashed into, made an exhibition of or simply left to get on with it. So just like being alive really.

Never let her go

A well-known saying is 'out of sight, out of mind', and I guess not everyone likes the idea; it would explain the need some people feel for a mausoleum, a headstone with flashing lights, or an LCD-screen message with a motion detector that triggers a 'Psst, hey you' when anyone walks by. It might also explain why a firm in Salt Lake City, Utah offers a modern form of mummification for more than a few thousand dollars. Included in the price is a bronze sarcophagus, which you're welcome to bury like any other coffin, but since no one who has signed up has yet died (though they have proven the process on pets) I'm thinking that this too is going to be more of an above-ground option. A huge bronze sarcophagus, that's just got to go somewhere between the Shaker-style bookcase and the 60-inch plasma TV, hasn't it?

While we're talking about the dead coming in from the cold, what of those who are willing to pass on to the undiscovered country but are kind of keen to have a return ticket? The answer is cryonics, or cryogenics – the big chill. The technology appears to be there; we can freeze and thaw living sperm cells, so why not the whole body? Well, for one thing, of those thawed-out cells 40 per cent are useless. But, you may be thinking if you're frozen that's at least a one in two chance you might be able to be brought back to life eventually, which is much better odds than, well, death. And there are supposedly somewhere around a hundred people in the US alone who are already frozen because they like those odds. A company in Riverside, California already has 35 chilled-out clients. For years rumour had it that Walt Disney himself was frozen, and, true or not, it does sort of have that 'Magic Kingdom' feel to it. It is true, however, that US baseball legend Ted Williams checked in for a little cryonic suspension, or suspended animation, rather than checking out. But here's the rub, it's just his head.

Of course, it's not merely the freezing process that's rather on the expensive side; keeping you frozen afterwards is pretty pricey too. The US institutes who provide this service charge from $28,000 up to $150,000 plus a yearly sum, starting around the $100 mark, for 'maintenance'. So you get the choice: to have your whole body frozen, upside down, to be revived at some time in the unspecified future when science is capable of repairing the damage done by the freezing process, or, the cheaper option, to have just your head frozen. Presumably the unspecified future for your head will need to be in a time when you have the choice of being attached to a body donor, a bio-robotic carcass or your own biogenetically re-grown body. Simple.

The process itself involves being instantly packed in ice the moment you die and your blood and other body fluids swapped for a sort of glycerine-based anti-freeze. Finally the patient is liquid nitrogened down to -195 degrees Celsius.

There are a few final points to consider before you rush willy-nilly to sign up to be a human ice cube. Firstly, even your home freezer requires power so you'd better make damn sure you pay this particular electric bill. Secondly, many of the people being frozen are those science geeks who truly believe in such a fantasy future, and would you want to wake up to a world where they were not only proven right but are the ones in charge? And lastly, the theory is that the whole cryonic process will have much more chance of success if the head is removed before death. Yes, that's *before* death!

There are now opportunities to chill out in Canada, New Zealand and England, as well as the US. However, since this technology is not only in its infancy, thus many of the practitioners are self-taught, and is also subject to the whims of the free market economy, you have to ask yourself what happens when one of the providers goes bust, such as the Cryonics Society of California. Not so keen on going all Austin Powers now, right?

And if you're still not dissuaded, let me tell you about Frozen Dead Guy, or Grandpa Bredo. It seems an immigrant from Norway to Nederland, Colorado USA, built a cold house in his garden in which to store his previously cryogenically frozen father. For various reasons, the son ended up being deported back to Norway, leaving his frozen dad behind. Now did they let him thaw and inter him? No. Did they ship him back to Norway? Again, no. What they did do was hire someone to maintain his chill and turn him into a tourist attraction. The local economy is now boosted by Frozen Dead Guy tours and an annual Frozen Dead Guy Day. The yearly event includes coffin races and a lookalike contest, won incidentally in 2005 by a visiting Belgian man.

If it's the will to live every possible moment we can that propels us into considering being a fish finger for eternity, then it's probably the inability to let go that leads to some people, well, not letting go. Yes, we all feel we want to keep some memento or reminder of our departed loved one. I might even acknowledge the urge to hold on to their ashes in an urn on the shelf, but actually keeping the whole body is really going far too far. Maybe it was the sadness of losing his wife of many years on Valentine's Day, but a 74-year-old man from Edinburgh in Scotland placed his dead wife in the freezer at their holiday home in Berwick-upon-Tweed, Northumberland where the police found her some 12 days later. The really strange thing is that he took her there by taxi, some 50-odd miles, and the taxi driver didn't even notice.

At least she found her eternal peace eventually, which wasn't the case for the wife of a guy from Arizona, USA, who confined his wife in a vacuum-sealed glass coffin he uses as a coffee table. Allegedly there's a 17-year-old Vietnamese boy who spent 38 years in a coffin in his family home after a medicine man told his father he wasn't dead. And on the French Indian Ocean Island of Réunion the body of one particular Madame is being kept on ice until the battle between her children and the French authorities over their desire to keep her in a glass freezer at home is finally resolved.

You have no such problem, however, if you happen to be a South African farmer from KwaZulu-Natal province who keeps his embalmed wife in a self-built air-conditioned crypt wearing her favourite nightdress. There's even a door in the coffin that opens on her face. Okay, I'm going to move now, it's all getting a bit too Norman Bates for me.

Top ten things to do when you're dead

1. *Get stuffed:* There has to be a taxidermist out there who'd just love a challenge. Have him, they usually are male, either pose you sitting so you can return home to your favourite chair, or standing up so that your family can move you around as they redecorate.
2. *The final frontier:* If you've always been a speed freak and the idea of being a crash-test dummy actually appeals to you then at least try to donate yourself to the space programme.

3. *It's magic:* Why not will yourself to the Magician's Circle for them to practise their knife-throwing and cutting-people-in-half tricks on?

4. *Plastic people:* Let the good German doctor plastinate you then donate yourself to your favourite bar to be placed up there with the music memorabilia, the wooden Indian and the reproduction sporting goods.

5. *Food for thought:* Donate yourself to a willing zoo as food for your favourite carnivore; tell them it's instead of a sponsorship for Lenny the lion.

6. *Wooden:* You could always audition for a part on a day-time soap opera.

7. *Go to sea:* For the nautically inclined, why not offer yourself for the role of figurehead on a sailing ship?

8. *Not so dead:* It seems being dead doesn't preclude you from still receiving junk mail, cold calls or voting in certain countries, so why not live on in a virtual plane?

9. *Believe:* Have your lifeless body taken to a faith healer to see if they like a challenge.

10. *Exhibition:* Why not have yourself sneaked into a museum of modern art and see how long it takes for them to work out you're not actually an exhibit?

Chapter 8

The Wake: See and Be Seen

There's a common phrase 'I wouldn't be seen dead in ...' and it seems that what we wouldn't be seen dead in is a coffin, since the tradition of viewing of the dead is fading fast in many Western quarters of the globe. There was a time when we all venerated our dead in the way the Koreans or Buddhists still do by paying our respects to the physical body of the deceased. We call it a visitation, a viewing, a wake, or if you happen to rule a country – lying in state.

The English term 'wake' derives from the actual practice of keeping watch over the corpse to make sure it did indeed deserve to be called a corpse. Our forefathers couldn't always be sure they'd diagnosed death correctly, but then you've already read that chapter, haven't you? The Jewish tradition was to even provide special benches for the vigil; it can be tiring waiting for the slightest twitch, not to mention pretty much of a trauma if you spot one. Thus the wake was a ritual final check that the deceased really had ceased to hold on to life – kind of like the way we check every door and window is locked, that all the appliances are turned off and that we've got our keys before we leave the house. Or is it just my wife who insists I do that?

However, if it were only ever about looking for life after apparent death then you'd only really need to hire someone to go in and poke the stiff occasionally – the grandchildren would probably do it for free. So there had to be other reasons why such a ritual became ingrained into the death rites of societies the world over. Well, for one thing, religion got involved and the wake came to mean a watch to make sure that the deceased was left unmolested to 'wake' up again in the afterlife, though in other parts of the world the vigilance was a must to ward off body snatchers. And in certain mountain states in the US they were protecting the dead from rodents, insects and cats. Apparently cats were known to make off with the odd finger or two. See, that's why I'm a dog person.

It is likely that the warding off of both evil spirits and the evil living during the night would have required the use of lighted candles, not only to pierce the dark but to singe the wings of the demons. And, since the Church is no fool, it is more than likely the use of candles was incorporated into the less heathen and more religious version of the night watch – the reverential wake. If they were going to sell the idea of an afterlife it would help their cause to make a big thing of the whole passing from this land to the undiscovered country. So the more elements to the wake, the more important seemed the afterlife entry requirements. Thus the paying of respect to the dead, and of offering sympathy to the family along with the equally ritualised preparing of the body for interment – you know, washing, shaving, dressing, that sort of thing – meant that the wake came to last up to anything from an all-nighter to three or more days. And if you then add drink to the ritual it isn't hard to understand how in many parts of the world the wake took on something of a party atmosphere. In sub-Saharan Africa for example, it wasn't uncommon for naked fevered dancing to accompany the mourning, while in Ireland there was a time where the dancing even had something of a drag element to it.

And like all good parties there came a time for games, either around or involving the body. Pin the tail on the body may have been popular, or hide and seek, and the deceased would have won hands down at statues. The Irish would frequently play card games, and deal the guest of honour in.

The moving of the wake or visitation from the family home to the funeral director has meant that the practice, with much of its fun and gaming, is not as common as it was. That's not to say it doesn't happen; the three-day drink and song-fuelled wake is still one the highlights of an Irish funeral, though the equally wet wakes of the Australians and New Zealanders now take place after the funeral itself, no doubt because that way they're pretty confident that they're not going to bury anyone alive. These days many of us have removed ourselves so far from the death process that any visit we do pay to our dear departed is likely to take place in the antiseptic coldness of a funeral home.

So all kudos to the funeral home in Cleveland, USA where the owner has decked out the visiting room as if it were simply a normal bedroom; the casketless body is laid out in a comfy bed, and easy chairs are provided for the relatives to sit on. I suppose it's the ultimate in what's called an open casket viewing.

The Armenians and Georgians use the visitation to place small coins on the chest of the body, usually as a gift towards funeral expenses. In the southern hemisphere on Sulawesi Island the visitation means bringing gifts of live pigs or buffalo trussed under bamboo poles, which they then allow to fight or run free among the mourners before they are killed and feasted upon. The human members of the wake then dance in a circle around the dead for hours fuelled by the food and drink they have provided.

The powerful or famous are more likely to have open casket visitations then most – it's a chance for their public to say a final goodbye, as well as their friends and relatives. During the viewing of Bela Lugosi (the guy who played Dracula), Peter Lorre and Vincent Price (two other stars of countless Hollywood scary movies) came to see his casket. Lorre saw that Lugosi had been dressed in his famous Dracula costume and said to Price, 'Do you think we should drive a stake through his heart, just in case?'

The Wall Street financier John A Mulheren chose to lie in state – you get to call it that if you've got money – wearing a bright red suit, and was lucky enough to have Bruce Springsteen perform 'Santa Claus is Coming to Town' during the wake.

From the sublime to the, well, less sublime: the funeral wishes of an old Taiwanese gentleman led to something of a quandary for his family when he asked for a stripper to perform at his funeral. Not wanting to disrespect him, but also not really wanting such a public display at the funeral, the family eventually plumped for having the striptease take place during a private visitation. I only hope they didn't spoil it for the old fellow by having a closed casket viewing.

The closed casket is the alternative to having an open casket: but don't you think, unless there are really good reasons for keeping the lid on it – disease, disfigurement or just plain ugliness – bidding farewell to a closed casket is sort of saying goodbye to a box? At least if you have an open casket you can spot, like the family at one particular South African funeral, that it's the wrong body.

The ultimate in the open casket style takes place in some parts of Russia and Georgia where the coffin isn't closed until moments before the burial. At the other end of the spectrum are the Germans, as it's common custom in some regions of Germany not to have a viewing at all in their funeral homes. So the Germans have adopted the old 19th-century practice of having the deceased's photograph taken. Oh yes baby, that's it – the camera loves you!

The top ten no-nos at the open casket

1. Don't pinch his cheeks just to make sure.
2. Don't ask the woman behind if she knows what colour of eyeshadow that is.
3. Don't praise the undertaker for a great job because 'Isn't his other arm still in the thresher somewhere?'
4. Don't take something from inside the coffin as a souvenir.
5. It might be the done thing to kiss the deceased one last time but this doesn't mean tongues.
6. If the widow is stood beside her husband's coffin, the last thing you should be saying is, 'So, are you free tomorrow night?'
7. One last drink together from your hip flask, I don't think so.

8. Don't check to see if he's got his wallet on him, because he still owes you that 50 you loaned him.
9. Even if you have a hand mirror with you it's not done to test for signs of breath.
10. And this is really not the time to high five the widow about the will.

Chapter 9

Fusion Funeral: the Service

All in order

In English-speaking countries – the US, Canada, the UK, Australia and New Zealand – the funeral has become either less religious or more religious, it depends how you choose to look at it. Less than a quarter of Britons say they want a religious funeral now, and there's even been a swing towards a less deity-centred service in the US, especially in California. The world has seen a move away from single denominational religious services with the standard two hymns, a couple of prayers, a few words about the deceased and a lot of grief, to a more celebratory pick-and-mix type of ceremony. People these days want it very much their own way.

The fashion is to cut and paste anything that appeals from the major and minor religions and re-write them to your own idiosyncratic template, adding a healthy bit of paganism or the secular along the way, in order to create a sort of post-mortem potpourri. Thus at 21st-century funeral events you might very well be handed a personal computer printed order of service, on which you will see perhaps a sparse Quaker prayer, followed by the singing of 'Bohemian Rhapsody' by Queen (the words being on the back of the sheet), after which there will be a Native American or Druidic death chant (the front row being provided with Cree Indian rattles to shake in accompaniment), then it's eulogy time, followed by the local unsigned band playing their indie/garage/funk crossover version of 'Flying Without Wings' by Westlife (dry ice optional) and finally the deceased will be renamed Skychild Moonvoyager in a crib from the traditional Japanese Buddhist rite of giving the dead a new identity for their afterlife.

All the world's a stage

Since the funeral seems to have become more of a performance than a service the first thing people might do is to dress the stage. At its simplest that could mean having a life-size photograph of the deceased to greet the guests as they enter the chapel or arrive at the graveside. Asante funerals in Ghana place painted portraits and sculptures on the grave, and elsewhere in the world, and in the US naturally, the whole chapel can be decked out with enlarged photographs of those who have passed on.

A simpler idea from the States is that of the celebration box filled with treasured mementos of the recently flatlined. The family usually fills the box with photos, jewellery, medals, concert tickets – anything that has special significance from the life now extinguished. The funeral guests can then add their own objects to the box as they arrive at or leave the funeral, dropping in little notes, poems or the chainsaw they always meant to return after borrowing it ten years earlier. The beauty of such a box is that the bereaved will always have it as a remembrance of their loved one, and their family'll get their chainsaw back.

A variation on the box is to have items around the chapel that reflect the deceased's life, perhaps his work tools or items from her wardrobe or, if there's enough space, her shoes. It only matters that whatever you pattern the place with it, says Sheila, or Michael or Hans or Babs …

The mass sales of the high-end laptop might account for the funky new funeral trend of projecting a slide show of images of the decedent onto the chapel or church wall. It's quite common in both the US and the UK. Those who can make use of modern technology will do so and don't be surprised if you attend a first-world funeral and, instead of the order of service being pressed into your hand, each prayer, song, hymn and even a read-along version of the eulogy will hang there right in front of your eyes, courtesy of an overhead projector.

Fusion Funeral: the Service

Indeed, while you're reading, singing or chanting you should be even less surprised to see flashed images of the no longer with us via a slide or home movie show. The latter is particularly big in the States apparently. Even in parts of Germany, where it's still traditional to be traditional, you can expect to be handed a tiny photo of the deceased during the ceremony to personalise the process in some way. A shop in the south-west of England specialises in funeral ware and will supply you with lacquered photo albums to present to those who take photographs themselves during the ceremony.

In the US one Las Vegas funeral home has taken the whole idea of staging a funeral that one step further. Pictures and projections are fine but nothing compares to the whole 3D experience of a backdrop. A quick browse through their brochure allows you to select the cowboy experience, complete with wagon wheels, bales of hay, a cactus and even a plastic horse. They offer funerals with military, garden or kitchen trappings, though I'd hope the latter wouldn't be hired out for cremations too often. The golf option includes clubs, bags and course scenery, and since this is Vegas they can also let you take your final gamble surrounded by giant dice, cards and slot machines. Viva Las Vegas!

If you live in St Louis you have the option of a traditional kitchen setting with Wonder Bread, Crisco and real fried chicken and though they tell the funeral party that the food is merely a backdrop and not for consumption some of it will always go missing. If you think this might be all a little much, then consider the Sulawesi Islanders who build an entire village out of bamboo for the funeral guests to spend their time with a full-size effigy of the deceased, with the deceased's own hair. Of course in the West you're more likely to find real people with fake hair.

And if this still isn't enough to light up your cremation why not hire lookalikes of the famous – film stars or rock stars – to sit among the mourners? Just remember, if you do, it's best to stick to the living. Having an Elton John or a Sean Connery at your funeral will get your guests talking; having a Marilyn Monroe or a John Wayne will kind of give the game away and may even freak some people out.

Of course you don't have to have your memorial service at the chapel or graveside, you could do what a certain B T Collins, a former California state legislator, did when he hired a hotel ballroom and played out the final funeral performance on a much bigger stage to a much larger audience. Despite the fact that the room was filled with balloons, had a live band playing and the buffet even boasted an ice sculpture, there was no doubting the centrepiece of the show, B T Collins himself.

Not everyone has the foresight or capital to cater for 3,000 mourners but that doesn't mean the separation of the service from the actual interment isn't becoming a more frequent option. Golf courses, night clubs and sports grounds, professional and amateur, are all being pressed into use as backdrops. This all seems to hark back to the days of the grand funeral and putting on a show, but since this is the interactive age some of the dead are taking it the extra mile and inviting their family and friends to join in what has now become the celebration.

Themed funerals are getting especially big. You choose a theme relevant to yourself and ask everyone to dress for the funeral with that in mind. *Star Trek* funerals are up there at the top of the list and they are pretty easy to do since most costume-hire shops will keep several Starfleet uniforms; just make sure you don't beam in to the service wearing the red shirt, you might not beam out again. Other popular themes include the Prohibition Era, complete with violin cases, and various historical periods from the Arthurian legends to the Second World War; again costumes are fairly readily available from hire shops, theatrical costumiers and re-enaction societies.

There are those for whom the theme is rather more personal and maybe reflects a time when that person was in their pomp: the 50s, 60s or 70s, perhaps. Of course as we all grow older soon we'll have more examples of 80s dress funerals with mourners wearing jackets with their sleeves rolled up and leg warmers.

If you're worried that all this might overexcite your children into running around and screaming at the tops of their voices, there's no need to worry if you live in Santiago, Chile as you simply choose the cemetery with the crèche.

The big entrance

The stage is set, it's time for the deceased's big entrance high on the shoulders of six pall-bearers slowly pacing their way to the altar or graveside. If they've gone for the themed idea, this could be four or six men in pinstripe suits and fedoras or it could be six Arnold Schwarzeneggers, though it might simply be relatives or friends of the main man or the official pall-bearers who work for the undertaker. Remember, it will be cheaper if you don't hire the professionals. Whichever half dozen it is, there's an old rule from the golden days of Hollywood; the good guys enter from screen right and the bad guys enter from screen left, and, well, if you're superstitious it might be worth bearing that in mind. Another thing to consider when choosing pall-bearers is height. The funeral director will have six big strong fellas of pretty much the same size, if you decide to go with relatives and friends they may not be any of the above. It only takes one uncle or cousin shorter than the others for momentum to have a devastating effect on proceedings.

Fusion Funeral: the Service

If it's a regular, standard funeral then the carrying in of the casket is normally accompanied by the deceased's choice of music (more of which later) and the pall-bearers should remain reverentially silent. Some people just can't resist, however; Dillingham and Ziegfeld, two of the great Broadway producers, were pall-bearers at the funeral of the world-famous escapologist Harry Houdini. Dillingham is supposed to have whispered to Ziegfeld as they shouldered the coffin, 'I bet you $100, he ain't in there!'

The arrival at the grave or altar is frequently the last chance for people to say a final farewell to the checked out one. It's common for the bereaved to file slowly past the open coffin with a word or two to send him/her on their way, and in Italy it is sometimes the time for one last kiss goodbye. In Eastern Orthodox religions the casket is usually opened one final time for this purpose just before the interment, while in parts of the Congo it has become a recent custom to touch the decedent to show you had nothing to do with his or her death.

In Western countries this is also the point in the proceedings where the mourners are more and more frequently being asked to sign a book of condolence; it's like a hotel reception book, though you're not really allowed to make negative comments, even if you do use a false name – it doesn't matter if he promised to leave his wife for you for the last 15 years, this is not the time to make it public. The other thing it isn't is a suggestion book – you're hardly likely to endear yourself to the family with comments such as 'You do a great funeral, when are you going to do it again?'

It's not always possible for the casket to be open for this ultimate goodbye – see earlier for some pretty good reasons – and it seems that people have now adapted the Jewish ritual of placing stones on the tomb in honour of the dead. Instead of stones, funeral guests are being asked to place flowers, a token, a note or a card on top of the coffin. In the south-west of England you can even buy handmade paper notebooks to hand out to the funeral party in case they've forgotten to bring their own. 'Token' has also come to mean many things, such as the deceased's favourite childhood toy, perhaps a model car or teddy bear, to the more bizarre, such as a whip or a pair of handcuffs. At the recent funeral of Freddie Garrity, the lead singer of the 60s beat group Freddie and the Dreamers and well known for his clowning around, the coffin was topped off with a jester's hat.

Once everyone has regained their seats, depending on whether the corpse had a wicked sense of humour and gave final instructions to have one of the seats taken away, forcing the mourners to play a swift game of musical chairs, and yes, it has been done, then it's time for the service itself to begin.

In your own words

Funeral directors have seen the way the funeral world is turning and most now are willing to at least listen to your requests. So in Great Britain if you wish to replace the common prayer with a white witch binding spell then you got it. Though I somehow doubt many establishments outside of Thailand would be quite so open to the idea of following the first hymn with a striptease by girls hired from the local bawdy-house. And they might also advise the widow that a straightforward eulogy might go down better with her late in-laws than the detailed descriptions of the virility of the deceased to be heard at funerals in the Mulian region of that area of East Asia. And, if you do somehow manage an invitation to such a funeral, you may also find that the home movies of the deceased you may have experienced elsewhere have been transformed into a pornographic video show. Each to his own, I say.

Another area of the standard service under threat is that of the reading from a religious text, which is now often replaced by a poetry reading. The most widely read poems in the English language are those to do with death and funerals (well, obviously) and include verses by W H Auden, especially 'Funeral Blues' after its starring role in the movie *Four Weddings and a Funeral*, and those by Robert Burns and Dylan Thomas. Thomas goes down particularly well in Wales, where it's almost obligatory to have a round-voiced mourner, who fancies himself the local bard, try to do a Richard Burton 'Do not go gentle into that good night'.

The selection of poem isn't always quite so apposite however, since the modern funeral is all about personal choice. And if the horizontal one wanted a reading from Shakespeare then it well might be 'Out out, brief candle' but it might also be the increasingly requested Saint Crispin's Day speech from *Henry V*, you know, the one with the 'we few, we happy few' in it, popular because of the 'band of brothers' line that links it to the popular Second World War TV series, thanks to Stephen Spielberg.

And if you're looking for something a touch more humorous, might I suggest 'Bump Starting the Hearse' by Kit Wright?

A growing international trend is for a member of the family to write their own little poem and read it, or have it read out at the service, and who among us wouldn't be moved to tears by the quivering lip and welling eyes of pigtailed seven-year-old Amy reading the verses she wrote about her granddad because she was always riding high on his shoulders and smelling his neck smeared with Old Spice? Okay, me for one, but then I cringe easily.

A quick google will show you that there's even no need for you to pace the Persian carpet yourself struggling to find a rhyme for botulism. There are literally hundreds of poets out there, mainly in the US, willing to write you a series of rhyming couplets all about your dear departed parent or wife or cat, if you pay enough. You can actually get someone else to personalise the whole service for you if you wish, if that's not paradoxical.

Britain, Australia and the US have recently seen the rise of the humanist celebrant who will help arrange the secular funeral of your late family member. They'll chat to you about the deceased, find out what kind of person he/she was, if they loved animals, if they were members of the local gym, if they liked to be called Big Pop and bounce their grandchildren on their knee, that sort of stuff. They'll use the answers you give them to put together a eulogy they can then deliver for you if you wish. They'll even help you choose and source the music, location and any other special requests you might have. The British comedians Ronnie Barker, Dave Allen and Bob Monkhouse all had humanist funerals, I guess so they could hear laughter one last time.

In the US the certified funeral celebrant is as equally in demand, though they are more willing to let a little religion sneak into proceedings if it's your wish. Richard Pryor, actor and comedian, left this place with a funeral celebration, and the celebrant even managed to include his trademark expletives in the eulogy. And though we can all opt for the video montage that Pryor had as part of his funeral if we've got enough home movies or DVDs, most of us won't have Diana Ross singing 'Amazing Grace', will we?

There was a time, not so long ago, where the taping of a funeral to watch later was considered ghoulish. You had to hide your super-8 movie camera inside your coat and that restricted the view and muffled the sound, or so I'm told. The fact that many funerals are now more of a joyous celebration of a person's life means that not only has recording events stopped being a reason to be asked to leave but has become one of the top items on the funeral 'to do' list; book church, order coffin, buy/borrow/hire DVD recorder. At some Ghanaian funerals each of the guests is actually given a copy of the day's proceedings, sometimes as they leave.

Don't be surprised if the next funeral you go to is a sea of mobile phones recording the best bits, all their owners secretly hoping something funny happens so they can send it in to one of those home-video TV shows.

And exits

There's nothing like a big finish and whether it's time for the lowering of the coffin into the grave, or the pressing of the button that begins the casket's final glide towards the furnace, well, there's nothing like going out with bang. If you're in the military there are, literally, several bangs, depending on your rank.

Throughout the world, the lighting or more often the snuffing out of candles is perhaps a poll leader when it comes to those final moments, but it isn't the only way to go. In certain German towns the tolling of the passing bell is stopped at exactly the moment the coffin is lowered in the earth, followed by the tossing into the grave of the attendant flowers by the oldest daughter. Funeral services in the US and the UK now have climaxes that involve the releasing of balloons or white doves, or in certain parts of Yorkshire the deceased's homing pigeons. It's not uncommon in both countries to set off fireworks, mostly rockets, just in case.

Expensive funeral flowers can now serve a dual purpose and be strewn over the grave or pyre. One English committal ended with the raucous last post of kazoos, whistles and party poppers, while another gothic-themed event climaxed with the funeral guests setting fire to their late friend's caravan. Though even they would find it hard to top the US amateur illusionist who is supposed to have hired one of his professional brothers to cover his coffin in a cape and whip it away at the climax of the service and reveal that the coffin was gone.

The end of the service at a New Orleans funeral signals the formerly dirge-like music to get with the beat and hit the joyous notes for the congregation to dance and wave their hats, umbrellas and handkerchiefs too. The hanky part is to show that there's no more need for tears. And the thing is you don't have to live in New Orleans to have a Mardi Gras-style funeral, you can even be deposited to the strains of a jazz band in the shadow of Hadrian's Wall, England.

Food for thought

No funeral would be complete without the ritual offering of food to the mourners. Or indeed the food may be provided by the mourners themselves, as is the case in the poorer, more rural areas of Europe, such as the east. They mostly contribute home-made stuff, as turning up with a can of something you had stuck at the back of a shelves somewhere and asking if anyone thought to bring an opener, well, it's not so tactful.

The funeral feast can be a before, during or after event, depending on where you live and local tradition. In many African countries the body cannot be buried until the feast is over and the food runs out, which can take up to three days. Of course the Irish wake takes place before the actual service and it too has been known to last three days on occasion – a tradition shared by American Gypsies who also break bread with the dead before the committal. Our friends the Sulawesi similarly feast on pork and rice, and indulge in rice wine before the interment of their dead.

An eastern European tradition, that has travelled as far as the Sudan and beyond, is to have the meal at the graveside with the deceased so that they can join in, well, not perhaps there and then but later when the food given to them during the feast, or left for them after it was over, is turned into soul food by the prayers. The Solomon Islanders do this by pitching the food onto a fire lit for the dead. Some peoples even pour a drink of wine into the grave for the chief guest, though if you're a non-believer it must seem like such a waste.

Obviously the feast must take place during the interment if you're a cannibal culture such as certain New Guinea or Amazon tribes. It hasn't always been the flesh of the deceased that's been the main course of the banquet either, as the Tartars were supposed to have eaten parts of those slain by their leaders, who had themselves died in battle, at their funerals. I'm kind of glad that one died out.

The tradition in the Western world is, for the most part, to have the supper after the funeral service itself is over; food is served and tales are told of the exploits of the deceased. In Britain there has long been a tradition of serving a ham, and offering tea to the guests. Other cultures have their own specific funeral food. In parts of Europe, particularly Belgium, they have soul cakes, based on the age-old simnel cake. In fact the traditional Belgian funeral has a sort of sepia feel to it, with soul cake covered in dark-coloured icing, served on a black fretted paper doily and accompanied by white wine. In Africa it's the done thing to slaughter a cow for the feast, though if you're Amish you'll be quite content with a raisin pie. Or maybe your taste is for the funeral potatoes served, though not exclusively so, at Mormon funerals. It'll also come as no surprise that the Turks serve lokum, or Turkish delight, during their funeral suppers.

So from the traditional to the modern, and as with the rest of the service becoming more individual so comes the pick-and-mix funeral supper. There are now catering companies who will serve your specific needs when it comes to laying on a spread. The choice is frequently to serve the deceased's favourite foods and if that means jellied eels in the old East End of London or a huge rack of Texas-style BBQ ribs in Texas, then you've got it. There's also a growing trend to serve takeaway food at funeral feasts, even in Africa, and it can't be too long until you can order a funeral feast chicken bucket, or have a selection of pizzas covered in the decedent's favourite toppings delivered to the graveside. No, wait, that's been done already.

For those who still want to take part in the total funeral experience there are now even cookbooks on the market with assortments of recipes for after-death food. The English food writer Nigella Lawson has such a section in one of her books.

And when it comes down to it, the main thing about the western funeral is – no matter how much you didn't like the guy, or can't remember the woman – hey, the food's free!

Memento mori

What if you've enjoyed the fusion funeral so much you didn't want it to end? If you go to the theatre or a rock concert you can buy a programme or a CD or DVD of the event, and now you can have the same lasting experience from your favourite funeral. A company in Ohio, USA offers you a grieving pin in the form of a black folded ribbon with an optional faith symbol. You can wear it to the funeral and then again afterwards to show you were there. I suppose it's like a Grateful Dead tour T-shirt for the real dead. And you're only following a tradition that goes back hundreds of years to the medieval mourning ring; if they were good enough for Anne of Cleves and William Shakespeare, who are we to scoff at the idea?

Since rings always have been, and will be, on the expensive side, other gift traditions have grown up in less affluent areas. In the north-east of England the mourners have formerly been given a sealed white paper parcel containing a slice of rich cake or a paper bag of biscuits, while in the Dutch East Indies the doed koeks or funeral cakes handed out included the initials of the passed, perhaps to make sure you were at the right funeral.

Let's face it, cake and biscuits may have been fine in days gone by but in the age of Bluetooth, PvP and the iPod you wouldn't want to die of embarrassment by giving them out at your funeral now. Which is why firms in California and Florida offer a personalised documentary-style DVD of the deceased for the family and friends attending the funeral, compiled from home movies, photos, and cherished mementos, all tastefully narrated to 'ambient' music. One comes with an elegant figurine on a base, and the other with a choice of small, medium or large keepsake book.

If you're the kind who asks not what the dead can do for you but more what you can do for the dead, or at least for their family, then do what the Japanese, or certain sub-Saharan tribes do and bring them a gift of clothing or food. Food is also the theme of the Norwegian funeral gift of a cake with the iced initials of the decedent. In modern America you have the option of turning up with a grieving basket containing comfort food, chicken soup and chocolate; a teddy bear, a scented candle; or a caring-for-yourself audio book and some anger putty.

In China the tradition is to give the family of the deceased a plain white envelope with a small amount of money in it. Let me see, anger putty or money? No contest.

Can't be there?

There's normally a good reason why you can't attend a funeral, perhaps because you're not on the guest list and can't get past security. It needn't be a problem though if the organisers have installed huge speakers on the church or giant video screens nearby and broadcast a live feed to them, much as they did for the funeral of Alberto Sordi the Italian comic actor in Rome or the state funeral of Diana, Princess of Wales in London, though unlike in Rome for Sordi there was no chanting of Diana's name by the crowds. The funeral of Jimmy Zambo, Hungary's biggest pop star, was even shown live on a private television station, so it was almost like being there.

If distance is what keeps you from attending, then if your friend, colleague or relative is going to have their big day in Hull (in England), Karachi (in Pakistan) or California (in the US) modern technology can come to your aid, as all these places now offer a live internet feed for funerals performed at certain cemeteries there. The US site provides a page to accompany the web-cast that lets the family give details of the service, upload photos of the deceased (while alive hopefully – or that would be a very different kind of website) and a section for personal messages. If you're thinking of attending a cyberfuneral, it's probably best to have broadband to allay any worries about the buffer crashing, and you get the added bonus that you can burn it to DVD if you so wish. Actually it doesn't even have to be the funeral of anyone you know, you might just be into that stuff.

Should you be one of the people not on the Internet, and I'm assured that they exist, then a company in the US has created a system that allows you to dial a certain telephone number where you will be connected to the service live. Press one for cremation, press two for burial or press three to speak to a deity …

If all this choice is a little too much for you, you could always move to Pensacola, Florida so that when the time comes you can simply drop the body off at the drive-through funeral home and have done with it, and maybe fries. Or maybe not, since at the time of this book going to press it had closed down. Perhaps some things can be just too fast.

Top ten examples of bad funeral service etiquette

1. It's bad form to hit on the widow; if you must offer your arm for support it should be gently around the shoulder only, not the waist, and even then the hanging hand should droop nowhere near the vicinity of the breast.

Fusion Funeral: the Service

2. If it is an open casket service, it just isn't done to slap your hand to your mouth as if you are going to toss your cookies.

3. If it's a graveside service, do not climb on nearby gravestones because you can't see what is happening.

4. If it's the funeral of someone from your firm, it is not a chance for a bit of networking.

5. Try not to forget if you are driving in a funeral procession and that maybe hitting your horn is a bad thing.

6. It's considered impolite to suddenly rush up to the crematorium curtains or hang over in to the grave because you've decided you actually want the token you put on the coffin back.

7. You should so not march to the front row of the chapel and ask the widow to budge over a bit.

8. It would be tactful not to admire the deceased's shoes and ask what size he was.

9. A funeral service is not the same thing as a wedding service at all; there is no place in the proceedings for the words 'I object'.

10. Never upstage the decedent at the service by dying yourself, that's such bad form.

Chapter 10

Funeral Fashion

All dressed up with somewhere to go

Yes, the traditional white shroud is still hanging around but the more we personalise the proceedings the more we move away from the so-called funeral norms. These days it isn't all black, black, black. Though the deceased can still wear black of course – in fact there are tailors in Poland who make their entire living from sewing just such funeral suits – the tailors in good old Samegrelo, Georgia will knock up the fantasy funeral outfit of your choice. And if that's what you want for your own funeral, just make sure you tell your family, especially if you live in certain areas of Germany where the custom is for the dead person's neighbours and friends to dress them for the funeral. It may sound pretty disgusting, but that's a breeze when compared to the tradition in parts of what was once the Soviet Union where the same people washed the corpse. And if that's still not repulsive enough yet: in some particular socialist republics you washed the body either after or just before death.

Those given such a task might do well to consider using the services of a seamstress in Fort Worth, Texas who sews simple one-size-fits-all post-mortem suits and dresses. The suits have fake flies and no pockets, tie up at the back and come with shirts and a tie already attached. (Although if you happen to be a professional wrestler, stripper or Chippendale you no doubt already own at least one pair of easy-on, easy-off trousers.) The same state also has a more upmarket funeral clothing designer for the more discerning corpse.

Another result of the rise of the individualised death ritual has been that the dead are now taking their eternal rest in outfits that had some meaning in their life. Military men have always had the option to be buried in their uniform, but those of other occupations are now being afforded the same choice. If you're a footballer or tennis player or athlete why not sleep the last sleep in your sponsored shorts, shirt and trainers/boots? However, if you're a golfer it's best to think twice about spending eternity in load flares and a sweater even your dad wouldn't wear in public.

Of course you don't have to be sporty to go to the grave in your work clothes; mechanics can wear their overalls, nurses their uniforms, teachers their dodgy ink-stained jackets with leather patches on the elbows, and S & M mistresses, well that's that other book again, which would

probably have to include the funeral of one US gentleman who lived off the earnings of his ladies' virtues. Okay,
he was a pimp and his former employees all attended his
funeral dressed and ready for business.

Another popular alternative is to wear an outfit that has
a special meaning to you. More and more football fans are
being buried or cremated wearing the colours of the team
they support. And not just soccer fans either. A woman
in Detroit, USA was buried in her beloved baseball club's
uniform in a coffin bearing the team's orange, navy and
white colours.

Maybe your outfit signifies your lifestyle, like the British
woman who went into that good night true to her gothic
sensibilities wearing the blackest of black denim jacket and
jeans to contrast with her white make-up and long painted
nails. Or maybe you simply want to go out wearing your
favourite outfit; your pulling suit, the little red dress that
always got you noticed or even that comfortable, if tattered,
old pair of jeans you somehow could never bear to part
with. In the UK the anti-pollution rules at least mean your
dad can't choose to forever lie in that awful white polyester
suit that he swore made him look and dance just like John
Travolta.

If you live in Ghana the one suit might not be enough
since it's become the fashion for modern corpses to change
outfits several times during the visitation and funeral as

not only a show of good taste but as a display of the dead person's wealth. The more ostentatious the display, the more respect garnered. I want to ask if they have a master of ceremonies to describe each new outfit but perhaps I'd better not.

It's enough to make you want to become a nudist. Well, you don't actually have to wear anything except your coffin, but if that's the case may I suggest a closed casket visitation? Koreans have found a less drastic way around the expense of a new outfit for the funeral by providing a hire service for both the guests and the body.

Guest fashions

Changes can also be seen in the fashions of those who attend funerals. The movement from sombre passing on to your choice of spiritual place to joyous celebration of the deceased's life has meant that dark clothing and dark moods don't quite cut it anymore. In a recent survey in the UK 89 per cent of those asked said their family and friends should wear bright colours to their funeral.

And equally in east and south-east Asian countries the choice of white raiments is giving some way to the black of Western influence, with – in a photo-negative version of modern US and European funerals – white armbands.

And In The End

Even the European aristocracy have moved on; HRH Prince Charles actually wore a blue suit to the state funeral of Princess Diana as it was her favourite. Blue to a royal state funeral is close to wearing bright orange to the funeral of your average mortal. Now suits of all shades and hues are acceptable if worn with a black armband.

I know what the more conservative of you are thinking: that it's only a small step from beige lounge suits to the total anarchy of the wear-what-you-like brigade with their dress-down Fridays at work, schools allowing sweatshirts as part of the uniform and restaurants letting you in without a tie. Where's it all going to end you're thinking – women being allowed to attend funerals in skirts and expose their bare shoulders? Actually yes, it's even common for them to show a little cleavage. Maybe it is the end of the civilised world as we thought we knew it. In the US it's the custom among the young, especially at the funeral of one of their own, to attend in jeans and trainers, and again it's the rise of the less formal celebration of life that is to be blamed or applauded, depending on your point of view.

In the US it's equally not uncommon for funeral guests to turn up to the service wearing baseball jackets loudly proclaiming the name of New York Giants, or any American or National League team, if that was where the deceased spent his down-time.

Funeral Fashion

As one funeral tradition dies, it seems another is born. And the new tradition? Funeral T-shirts. In the US you can brighten up the arrival of the deceased at the chapel by wearing a T-shirt with 'Always a Pall-bearer, Never a Corpse' emblazoned on it. The fun funeral 'T' may have its genesis in the Caribbean or West Africa where Ghanaian mourners, along with the traditional funeral colours of black, red and white, started wearing shirts, headscarves and handkerchiefs with photos of the deceased. Wherever it started, it seems to have spread first to Oakland, California, where an artist ran a one-man operation, and then on to New York, Miami, Chicago and Washington, where there are suppliers of 'RIP' T-shirts.

The airbrushed RIP often sits above a photo of the decedent, with the date and time of his/her death added underneath. Other slogans such as 'Gone but Not Forgotten' are also available. It doesn't stop there either; in Baltimore, USA young people can be seen at funerals wearing RIP sweatshirts, T-shirts, ties and baseball caps all depicting pictures of the deceased.

Is it just me or do you get the feeling that what goes around comes around? This seems vaguely reminiscent of the Romans wearing masks of their ancestors or later Italians processing photographs of the funeral guest of honour? It even seems, though most of us still prefer the guy in charge to be wearing his dress uniform so to speak, there's a growing trend towards those who lead civil ceremonies sporting civvies. The certified celebrant usually turns up to guide the service dressed smart but casual, at least in the US. In the UK there are examples of humanist celebrants arriving looking like a cross between a mad professor and a charity shop mannequin, though not all, I must stress. In England the late motorcyclist can even be officiated over by a vicar in full leathers, while if you live, or die, back across the pond why not have an Elvis conduct the last rites before the deceased becomes a hunk, a hunk of burnin' love?

Top ten funeral fashion faux pas

1. *To a T:* No matter how much you might be thinking it, put the T-shirt with 'Good Riddance' on it back in the closet.
2. *Snap:* A quick phone call to the bereaved could save you the embarrassment of being seen alive in the same outfit as someone being seen dead. And, who knows, you might even get a date out of it.
3. *No competition:* Remember the funeral is much like the alter ego of a wedding and it's not the done thing to upstage the bride or the corpse with your outfit.
4. *Any old suit:* Just in case you thought I was speaking merely to the ladies, the men should be aware that one

size doesn't fit all forever. The black suit you bought for your first ever funeral will not somehow miraculously grow as you do, nor, no matter how retro the world in general gets, will it come back into fashion – flares come and go but sleeves that bare the creases of constantly being rolled, not a chance.

5. *Listen very carefully:* When you get a telephone invitation to a funeral and the words 'dress' and '70s' are mentioned, make sure you don't confuse the guest of honour's age with the fancy dress theme.

6. *Magnum:* Hawaiian shirts – just don't.

7. *Uniform:* You may have only been allowed to attend the funeral on your lunch break but you should still try to find the time to change out of your fast-food outfit or, if you can't, at least remove your name badge.

8. *Fire:* If it's to be an open-air cremation, it's best to go easy on the hair lacquer.

9. *Skin:* Yes, the deceased may have been a nudist, but just check before you go, okay?

10. *No laughing matter:* You may think it funny, but not everyone will appreciate your sense of humour if you turn up dressed as the Grim Reaper.

Chapter 11

Say It With Flowers

Flowers can say a lot and there are three simple ways they tell the dead how we feel about them: in words, in images and in themselves.

The wreath can be made to spell out our feelings: 'Goodnight Granddad', 'Mum', 'Luv You' or 'Bastard!' Or you can give a message to the world, as the family of a British road accident victim did by having their wreath say 'SLOW DOWN' and displaying it in clear view through the rear window of the hearse. The more the funeral becomes a pick-and-mix, the more we're bound to move away from simple generic flower messages the likes of 'Dad' to individual salutations relevant to the deceased. It can't be long till we see the coffin of a Nike vice chairman accompanied by a wreath that reads 'JUST DID IT'. I'm not suggesting it; it just seems inevitable. Far be it from me to plant seeds in your mind that might blossom into flowers that spell out 'DEAD DAD – SPONSORED BY SUTTON AND SONS'.

If you're not a big one for the words, then why not have the wreath made to represent your loved one? The flowers can be shaped into a football for a fanatical fan, a dog for a departed pooch lover or trainer, a huge apple pie for a gastronome – actually this one can serve two purposes since it not only defines the person but gives us cause of death. The list of objects that somehow reflect the life of the deceased can be constructed from flowers is bound only by our imagination and the skill of the florist. However, if you live in China you don't actually have to bother with real flowers at all, you can send them 'virtually' over the Internet.

The language of flowers

Not so long ago almost all of us would have known the symbolic meaning of the gift of any particular flower. Our ability to talk the language of flora is slowly being lost. Yes, we all know that an orchid means I admire your delicate beauty and that a red rose means I want to get inside your thong, but we are conscious of precious little after that.

When it comes to funerals, it's good to remember that some people out there still retain the ability to speak fluent flower. Just think what you might be saying if you opt to send artificial blooms to the funeral, unless the deceased was an artificial person, spiritually or physically. It's best to send the fresh variety and it's got to be best to stick to the simple 'goodbye' of the cyclamen or the moving 'beautiful spirit' represented by the larkspur. When choosing your floral arrangement remember white carnations that signify 'remembrance' are fine, as is a sprig of rosemary for the same sentiment, but you don't want the yellow variety of carnation with their 'cheerful' message. Unless of course it's a secret code between you and the other members of the local horticultural society who strangely always finished behind the recently checked out in the annual flower show. A Casablanca lily will send the same message though it's probably too late if you're the 'secret admirer' represented by the yellow chrysanthemum, and perhaps your bouquet of yarrow, meaning 'good health', could have been sent a little earlier. And only if you are sure should you send a wreath completely formed of virginal white blooms, as, let's face it, today the odds are pretty much against you.

It's not only the flowers that have meanings; the colours you choose also have something to say. In astrology the colour that represents Libra is violet; the Native Americans use orange to show kinship; the Asians feel yellow helps ward off evil; and in the West gold is the symbol of wealth. So you could send a wreath com-

prising of all those colours, but then how many of us are related to wealthy half-Asian/half-Native American Librans in peril?

Then there's the accompanying card, your last chance to say a few parting words, or maybe something a little more personal, sometimes too personal. I recently heard the story of a weekend tennis player, a quiet unassuming chap with a loving wife and kids, who dropped dead during the final set. His doubles partner still refused to concede the game however – well, they were 4–1 up with a point to break again. The other players were grief stricken, after they'd finished 'discussing' the result. At the funeral the remaining three members of the doubles match started reading the sentiments expressed on the cards attached to the wreaths, as one does, and in amongst those from close family and friends were some in fine feminine script, attached to huge bouquets of red roses (see above). And the sentiments – let's just say your itemised telephone bill would include at least one premium rate call listing to find anything quite so graphic. It slowly dawned on the trio that the names signed above the copious kisses were rather redolent of the countries the funeral guest of honour visited on business.

What did they do? Like true gentlemen they discreetly removed the fruitier cards before the arrival of the funeral party and the widow, and drank a toast to their dear departed friend and were thankful he had had any energy to play tennis with them at all. And, of course, they couldn't help but play the 'Is she one?' game during the funeral supper. The point of the story – little cards can say a lot, maybe too much.

No flowers, by request

One of the phrases you may find in a funeral announcement is 'no flowers by request'. This isn't merely a whim of dead hay fever sufferers; it's a personal choice, and it's becoming a more popular one, if not with florists. Some people feel that they'd rather have their friends, and family's money spent on a good cause rather than an expensive wreath that will ultimately either wither and die or be disposed of less graciously somewhere.

When I say good cause, they frequently are: medical charities, animal charities, and scientific research projects – all very worthwhile and worthy recipients. That doesn't mean that sometimes the deceased or the surviving family members don't have a not-so-hidden agenda in asking for memorial gifts to be made in the name of the recently flatlined. For instance, the widow who asked for donations to be made to the local radical feminist's group in the name of her misogynist husband. Or the family of one crotchety old man, well known locally for bursting any football that came ever so accidentally into his precious walled garden, who asked for donations towards a local junior football trophy in the old bugger's name.

Some funeral invitations give guests the choice of donating to charity or sending flowers; there's even a third way – donating the flowers after the funeral. Once the party is over the flowers can be shipped to say a local residential home for the elderly or perhaps a nearby hospital to brighten up the place. If you go for this option, it's best to have the wreaths dismantled first. You really don't want a guy on the recovery ward who's just had a vasectomy to be handed a bunch of flowers saying 'Sadly Missed'.

Top ten unfortunate flower arrangements

1. *'Beloved Dad'*: Whether the DNA test results have come through or not, it's best to leave such wreath sentiments to the natural children.

2. *Recycling*: So you bought the patient a beautiful bouquet of flowers but then he went and died, and you don't want to waste them so have managed to keep them in water until the funeral? Fair enough, but just remember to check that you've replaced the 'Wishing you a speedy recovery' card.

3. *Shall I compare thee?:* It's traditional to view the collection of wreaths, either before or after the service, and while you're standing there it's also probably traditional to compare others' offerings with your own. However, it's always best to do so mentally – you never know who might be listening as you say, 'You'd have thought he could have afforded a bigger display than that, after all he's the one who's going to get most out of her will!'

4. *Donations:* If it's to be 'no flowers by request', remember your bookie is not a charity.

5. *Sadly missed:* This is fine in most circumstances, with the exception of the deceased who was trying to beat the world free-fall parachute target-jumping record.

6. *Toss:* It's probably best not to lead a chant urging the widow to throw the bouquet.

7. *Personal choice:* If you intend to hand the bereaved a bunch of flowers with the words 'I picked them myself' make sure you have a good head start on the person whose garden it was.

8. *Last minute:* Someone *will* notice if you try to grab a wreath from a nearby grave because you forgot yours.

9. *Back to nature:* Nobody wants to hear that you didn't bring flowers because they scream when their living roots are cruelly ripped from mother earth.

10. *Prickly:* A cactus? Just don't, okay!

Chapter 12
Getting There

In many countries around the world, especially in those countries that haven't yet moved their graveyards too far out of town, the on-foot funeral procession still thrives. The Chinese walk a banner before the cortège, carrying the name of the dead. In rural Taiwan it's traditional to process the body to its final resting place and it is something the entire village turns out for. These perambulations are accompanied by lavishly decorated floats crewed by the various families or artisans of the town or hamlet. In more recent times up to a third of funerals in Taiwanese villages have come to include scarcely clothed female exotic dancers in the procession. Their sexually charged gyrations are meant to distract the demonic spirits. But there's got to be some collateral distracting going on, right?

In Indonesia winged roofed biers are used to transport the coffin on the shoulders of men who dance and jump as they progress. And in Italy the procession normally takes place after the service and wends its way through streets lined with photographs of the guest of honour. Pity I missed Lola Ferrari's funeral.

By the by, one of the reasons suggested why modern motor funeral cortèges still travel so slowly is that they hark back to the days when all journeys of the deceased where undertaken by foot, or later horse-drawn carriage, and, whether during day or night, were accompanied by candles. It doesn't need much speed to snuff out a candle, unless they were using the everlasting comedy kind you put on birthday cakes.

Once, if you could afford it, the highly polished horse-drawn hearse, whether coach-built or a converted gun carriage, was your only option; these days it tends to be more often the choice of a country's royalty or its revered leaders, or maybe its new royalty – its celebrities. The Swedish author Astrid Lindgren, creator of Pippi Long-stocking, was drawn through the streets of Stockholm in such a hearse, followed by a lone white horse, as is their custom. You don't have to be rich, famous or royal to be thus drawn (though it helps), you just need the cash and you'll find there are funeral directors who keep a one-, two- or four-horsepower vehicle for those who want to take the last mile the old-fashioned way. It has great dignity and has the added advantage that you can leave one final gift for the roses of those who live along the route.

Getting There

For those who weren't so keen on horses, in the more remote parts of last-century Brittany a willow-covered farm wagon carried the corpse and was drawn by oxen – not quite so good for the roses. In years gone by in Norway sometimes neither the carriage nor the coffin could make it down steep-sided mountains and the deceased had to be moved by sled or strapped over the horse, which, you have to admit, sounds rather like the way the sheriff or bounty hunter used to bring in the bad guy in those Hollywood westerns of your childhood.

The modern motor hearse is the now the 21st-century people's transport of choice and comes with a surprising array of extras – just in case. These include umbrellas, wheelchairs, a video camera and, in the case of one London firm, a portable keyboard.

If you're in the mood for more retro transportation but don't want to risk quite such a huge traffic queue behind as at horse-drawn funerals, then the historic motor hearse is for you. In Sri Lanka you're likely to be taken to the grave in a converted Chevrolet station wagon, while in Australia one particular firm will supply you with anything from a 1927 Buick to a 1968 Holden hearse. In the US, for those fans of the Prohibition Era or *Some Like It Hot*, you can travel to your service in a classic gangster hearse; they might even throw in a little moonshine if you ask nicely.

But what of those who live their lives in the fast lane and for whom the idea of a standard hearse, classic or otherwise, all seems rather sedate? Well, a British undertaker may have just the thing to give a little extra oomph – a Harley Davidson motorbike and sidecar hearse. The coffin slides into the sidecar, naturally, they don't yet do pillion processions, and they advertise their deceased deliveries as slow, fast or very fast. They also understand brand loyalty and offer the options of a Triumph or Suzuki model, both of which are allegedly capable of 'doing the ton' if so requested. And it seems that even after death bikers can still manage to have one last run in with the law, as one of the Triumph hearses was pulled over by the police for its rider not wearing a crash helmet. The irony is while he was alive the sidecar occupant had never actually once been stopped by the police.

And motorcyclists are not the only group to have their own special hearse; for those off-roaders amongst us a Welsh firm will undertake to deliver you in a converted Land Rover 4x4. Perhaps it could come with a triangle in the rear window with a coffin logo and the words 'Body on Board', plus a bumper sticker that reads: 'If you can read this – you're next!'

Of course, you don't necessarily have to travel by hearse at all. A certain Wayne Rich in Putnam, USA made his final journey in a dump truck accompanied by the town fire engine, and Harold Peabody from Augusta proceeded to his grave aboard a hay wagon towed by his son driving a 1940 Allis-Chalmers RC tractor, followed by 16 other vintage models. Other US citizens have travelled the hardest yards in sanitation trucks, self-hire trucks and motor homes, and on the other side of the world inhabitants of the Caucases quite often accompany the coffin in the village truck decorated with flowers and twigs.

The more the funeral becomes a celebration of the man, the more the details of the funeral are asked to somehow reflect that man and so the mode of ultimate transport often represents the occupation of the deceased. Firefighters are carried by fire engines; shopkeepers delivered by delivery vans and undertakers taken by, er, hearses. In England an ice cream seller was wedged into his ice cream van and escorted by all the other ice cream vendors from the same area, all playing different tunes and confusing all the children who must have come bolting out of their houses thinking they were the ones who had died and gone to Heaven.

There is even the legend of a certain clown's funeral where, although the hearse was just a regular one and not one of those little clown cars where the doors fall off, when they arrived at the church a dozen other clowns in full costume squeezed out with the coffin.

The green funeral movement in the UK has seen a rise in the use of private cars to transport the coffin and its contents to the funeral, usually with the back seats folded down and a blanket on top for both dignity and so as not to shock passers by. It seems to be particularly popular amongst owners of Volvo estate cars or people carriers. The real trick is to get the deceased to the car without undue fuss or causing the good ladies of old London to swoon. English law requires that the body be decently covered, though, if there's to be no coffin, modesty suggests that the shroud be an all-over version.

As Great Britain is the birthplace of the train and the train spotter, it should come as no surprise that some people (and when I say people, I mean men) choose to take the train on one of the many private steam railways operating across the shires, such as the Keighley & Worth Valley Railway or the Midland Railway Centre near Ripley in Derbyshire. The latter offers transport to the steam train, travel in the brake van to the church, a toot on the whistle as a mark of respect and a funeral supper party on board afterwards.

In the 21st century there's also no reason why you should have to take that last journey alone. In England some of the self-service undertakers offer a bus to take along the family and friends and in Melbourne, Australia a company offers a minibus to take the casket and the 12 nearest and dearest to the cemetery in true Aussie style – it includes a DVD player, coffee facilities and even a mini-bar.

Getting There

The personalised funeral has also seen a change to the routes that the funeral cortège takes. In Ireland it's always been the custom to stop off at the deceased's favourite bars along the way to have one last drink to yer man, and one more last drink to yer man, and just another quick last drink to yer man. Now that custom has spread to many other corners of the globe; there's even a British version where the mourners stop off at the decedent's chosen café for a cup of tea.

In several parts of the British Isles the pace of modern life has led to cortèges being seen on motorways in order not to waste any time and allow the hearse to move on to the next funeral, and in the process we've seen the withering of some of the more interesting practices. At one time in Ireland if the funeral procession were to pass another church along its way it was required to circle it three times before continuing its journey, and there are a lot of churches in Ireland. In Yorkshire it was once thought the right of the funeral party to take the most direct path to the body's final resting place, even if that meant across someone else's land.

It's not unusual in our time for the coffin to be taken on something of a magical mystery tour of places that were important in the occupant's life: the schools they attended, their places of work, the park where they played as children and played with each other as teenagers. In Great Britain one lover of the horse racing, the sport of kings, had a circuit of the local racecourse included in the directions for his funeral cortège route.

Whatever form of transport you choose, things don't always run as smoothly as planned. Urban legends can be found worldwide of hearses having to stop and change a tyre, of hearses breaking down and having to be pushed by the mourners, towed by a breakdown truck to the funeral or even having to flag down a passing motorist and transfer the coffin. There are stories of funeral processions turning the wrong way down a one-way street or finding themselves in a dead end and having to back the entire cortège up. I'll leave you with perhaps my favourite (although unconfirmed) example that comes from the US and concerns a funeral director who made the mistake of loading the body first, then going back to pick up the funeral party five flights up in the apartment building. When they came back down the hearse, with body on board, had been stolen.

And one final word about making your way to your last home – apparently there's hardly an aircraft takes off without at least one coffin on board.

Top ten fantasy final journeys

1. *A mail van:* It might be quite fun to be delivered to your funeral, as long as you aren't delayed in the post.

2. *King Arthur:* One for the guys – to be rowed across a mist-covered lake accompanied by beautiful handmaidens; it doesn't get much better does it?

3. *A tank:* The perfect way to stop irritable motorists honking their horns at your funeral procession because you're going too slowly, with the added bonus it can fire off a round as a salute when you arrive at your destination.

4. *Dive, dive, dive:* If it's your choice to be buried at sea, why not get ahead of the game by starting out under water? Go by submarine and when you get there, simply let them fire your coffin out of one of the torpedo tubes.

5. *The magnificent seven:* Yes, it's a personal thing, but to take your last trip in a horse-drawn hearse driven by Yul Brynner and Steve McQueen, how cool is that?

6. *Route 66:* And maybe it's me again, but why not have your funeral procession take you past the houses of all your previous partners' houses, perhaps as the hearse stereo system blasts out 'Who's Sorry Now?'?

7. *Pimp my last ride:* There must be a low-rider hearse out there somewhere. Just think, you get to look cool

one last time with the added bonus that the constant jerking and rolling might just prevent you from being buried alive.

8. *Geronimo:* It may take a little practice and a few attempts, but how cool would it be to be parachuted into your grave?

9. *One for the ladies:* And I swear this was my wife's idea, a ride including pallbearers, baby oil, muscles and thongs. I have no idea what she means by that.

10. *Bowled over:* Since my wife got her choice in, my daughter had no wish to be left out and insisted she'd be quite happy being flushed down the toilet just like we did to her goldfish Monty.

Chapter 13
Mood Music

Music is one of the sections of the modern funeral service that is rapidly embracing change. In the search for something meaningful to play at a funeral there seems to be no limit to the contents of the jukebox. And why not?

The biggest death-tune jukebox is to be found in the West, and in the US and Europe most notably, because, as Mama Cass says, you gotta make your own kind of music.

It's not surprising that, since 21st-century society is trying to make the whole service more deceased-centred, we are choosing music that has something special to say to or about the decedent or to the congregation. And in the UK that means over 40 per cent of songs chosen are 'pop'. Whether pop, rock, easy listening or just plain weird, the choice of any particular song is made for many reasons: to put into words how we feel about the deceased, how they felt about life, to comfort us, or to actually cheer us up – though sometimes quite unintentionally.

Keep it live

It isn't necessary to have pre-recorded tunes at the funeral service; some people still opt for their music to be played live. In Ghana the funeral party sing along to drummers and flute players, while until recently in Estonia live music meant brass bands, though they still played mostly hymns with the odd waltz thrown in. The Native Americans sang and chanted, and at Irish funerals the fiddler and the piper were common accompanists. In fact the bagpipes are still the most requested 'live' instrument at British funerals, and are becoming increasingly popular in the US, even among those with no Scottish heritage whatsoever. And among the funeral fans of our favourite Samegrelo, Georgia, musicians can make a pretty decent living playing at services and wakes.

Other funeral music is played by the ubiquitous New Orleans Jazz Band, who are frequently asked to play 'When The Saints Go Marching In' (though logic dictates that the odds are against everyone whose funeral they play it at being a saint) and by string quartets, who are asked, less frequently is must be said, to play 'Heaven Knows I'm Miserable Now' by The Smiths.

Professional musicians aren't the choice of some. Many are deliriously happy with cousin Sally playing Pink Floyd's 'Comfortably Numb' on her recorder or allowing the local cleric to dust off his acoustic guitar for a rendition of 'Time of Your Life', the Green Day tune – possibly ignoring the fact that the actual title of the song is 'Good Riddance (Time of Your Life)', but then again maybe not. Matthew Sims, an employee of a funeral firm in Swansea in South Wales, will frequently be asked to lend his voice as an optional extra to the standard service.

If you live in the south of England you can hire the services of a particular guitar/vocalist who you can find on the Internet under 'Funeral Singer'. He'll play and sing along to backing tracks of many of the most commonly requested funeral songs, and has on offer a few of the more recent choices that haven't quite made the funeral charts yet but are still quite appropriate, such as 'Hero' by Enrique Iglesias, 'If Tomorrow Never Comes' by Ronan Keating and '(Everything I do) I do it for you' by Bryan Adams. You also have to admire the delicious irony behind some of the other options on his playlist: 'Mack The Knife' by Bobby Darin, 'Hello' by Lionel Ritchie or 'Wonderful Tonight' by Eric Clapton.

And just as there those who go down the do-it-yourself route by making their own coffins, writing and delivering their own eulogies and even growing their own flowers, so there are those who go the whole auteur hog and sing at their own funeral. Such was the case of one Brit who, for his cremation service, had made a recording of himself singing along to a karaoke backing track of 'Light My Fire'.

Sometimes even singing the theme tune to your funeral isn't enough for some; there are people who want to write the theme tune as well, or at least have it written for them. The marvellous Danish writer of fairy stories, Hans Christian Anderson, commissioned a march to be played as he was processed towards the church, instructing the composer that 'most of the people who will walk after me will be children – so make the beat keep time with little steps.'

There is one area where live music, of a sort, appears to be under threat and that is during the US military funeral where, due to a severe shortage of buglers, they are being frequently forced to broadcast a recording of the last post.

A touch of the classics

Extracts from classical pieces (most modern funerals don't last long enough to include the complete Wagner's Ring Cycle, even if some feel like they do) and popular arias are the choice of many dying Europeans. The Italians really go for Mozart, 'Requiem' of course, and the Finns and Spaniards just can't get their final rest without a little of Albinoni's 'Adagio For Strings'. In Norway top of the funeral pops is 'Time To Say Goodbye' by Andrea Bocelli or, for some reason, 'Viva Las Vegas' by the King, Elvis

Presley (not strictly classical I know but to anyone under the age of 30 it might as well be).

Though only 5 per cent of Brits opt for the classics, they are rather more eclectic than, say, the French who religiously stick to French composers. British choices include 'Nimrod' from Elgar's *Enigma Variations* and 'Jerusalem', Blake arranged by Hubert Parry, and, while these choices may be a touch nationalistic, they are leavened out by the choice of 'Ave Maria' by Schubert, Handel's 'Xerxes' or 'Nessun Dorma', Puccini.

In the US the martial music of Souza plays its part, but the more popular classic selections are those of Copland, and even 'Hoe-Down' from his Appalachian Spring suite. The great European composers are also well represented, no doubt due to the descendants of the mass migrations from the old world.

Play that funky music, white boy

A survey conducted across Europe in 2005 found that 40 per cent of the inhabitants of the British Isles now request contemporary or popular music at their own or their loved one's funeral services. I say popular and contemporary, as you can hardly call 'We'll Meet Again' by Vera Lynn contemporary since it hasn't graced the charts for about half a century. Nevertheless, it has suddenly popped into the funeral top 20 with a bullet, no doubt due to the end of the Second World War anniversary celebrations.

When it comes to choosing which discs to spin at their funerals, the English, Welsh, Scots and Irish are a predictable and loyal bunch. Bouncing around the top ten requested tunes for the past half a dozen years or so have been: 'My Heart Will Go on' by Celine Dion; 'Wind Beneath My Wings' by Bette Midler; 'I Will Always Love You' by Whitney Houston; 'The Best' by Tina Turner; and 'My Way' by Frank Sinatra (though some of music-nerd types insist on the original by Paul Anka).

Ever since the whole Princess Diana funeral bash you can hardly crash a UK funeral without hearing another outpouring of Elton John and 'Candle in the Wind'. Come on, show a little originality, please! They could at least opt for 'Funeral for a Friend' from the same album.

Other home-grown British selections are: 'You'll Never Walk Alone' by Gerry and the Pacemakers (which is the choice of both football fans and *Carousel* lovers); 'Angels' by Robbie Williams; and 'Always Look On The Bright Side Of Life' from Monty Python's *Life of Brian* (which has to be the way to go, you can't be sad and whistle at the same time, even the Danes and the Finns dig it).

Elsewhere in Europe apparently 20 per cent of those surveyed would opt for 'Show Must Go On' by Queen, who can also be heard rocking around the graveyards and crematoria from Sweden down to Spain with 'Bohemian Rhapsody', and 'Who Wants to Live Forever', with the Scots adding 'Another One Bites the Dust' and the English 'I Want To Break Free' to the Queen Rocks Your Funeral Compilation CD.

Any and all of the Queen corpse rock canon will go down well with the Germans, whose survey replies suggest that their future planting parties will have a heavy metal soundtrack. I understand the choice of Led Zeppelin's 'Stairway to Heaven', and I can handle 'Nothing Else Matters' by Metallica, but I seriously don't think I'd risk AC/DC's 'Highway To Hell'.

Aging rockers also come out top with the Swedish jury in the form of the Eric Clapton track 'Tears in Heaven', while the Danes are slightly more progressive in their choice of 'There is a Light That Never Goes Out' by The Smiths, but only if they can't have 'Om Lidt Bli'r Her Stille' by Kim Larsen. (Don't worry, it'll mean something to them.)

Further south around the still blue waters of the Mediterranean they prefer their death rock to be by dead people, as both 'Imagine' by John Lennon and 'Let It Be' by the Beatles (two of whom are dead) make the top of the lists of those countries with Latin-based languages.

Bubbling under to the west of Europe are: 'Without You', I'd like to say by Nilsson but more likely by Mariah

Carey, 'Memory' from the musical *Cats*, the King again with 'Always On My Mind' (probably because most Elvis fans are reaching that age) and 'Unforgettable' by Nat King Cole.

The problem with all of these songs is that they made the charts because they are a lot of people's selections, which, by the very nature of such a chart, means that they're actually making the funerals they are played at less individual. Thankfully there are those out there whose choice of tune is fervently idiosyncratic. Remember the lady from Detroit who met her maker wearing her baseball team uniform? Well, she went out to the sounds of 'Take Me Out to the Ball Game'. In Britain similarly obsessed soccer fans have gone to that eternal hospitality box in the sky to the strains of the words of a song doctored to make them relevant to their club. Some of the fans' songs need little change, such as the Birmingham City Football Club song 'Keep Right On To The End Of The Road'. Other fans have been known to request not so much a song as a chant; a sentiment less popular, I believe, with referees.

John Peel, a well-known DJ, presenter and columnist in the UK, had 'Teenage Kicks' by the Undertones played at his funeral, an ideal tune for all those men who go to the grave believing they had somehow managed to cling on to some semblance of their youth to the very last. Another British disc jockey, though a mobile one, chose 'Come on, Eileen' by Dexy's Midnight Runners as it was always the one song guaranteed to get everyone up and dancing, and he hoped for a similar effect at his funeral.

You have to admire the dead who were accompanied at their crematoria services by 'Hot, Hot, Hot' by Arrow or 'Hot Legs' by Rod Stewart. Equally laudable is a certain Maria who must have known the congregation would see the answer instantly to the question 'How Do You Solve A Problem Like Maria?' from the soundtrack to *The Sound Of Music*. Though, unless the name of your wife actually is Mary, it would be tactful to shy away from 'Arms of Mary' by the Sutherland Brothers and Quiver. Actually, talking of musicals, what was the guy who chose 'Reviewing the Situation' from *Oliver* trying to tell us?

Equally as idiosyncratic is the choice of 'Higher and Higher' by Jackie Wilson, the imagery of which cannot have been lost on those who attended the funeral where it was played, though the choice of Fontella Bass singing 'Rescue Me' was perhaps more than a little hopeful. Unless, of course, the person involved had something of a Chapter 3 phobia.

And, believe it or not, there are even those who depart this veil of tears to the inane beat of 'The Birdy Song' – one can only hope without the accompanying dance.

Then there are those who choose the theme tune to their favourite television show; thus in England services have taken place where the coffin has arrived to the sound of the music to popular soap operas *Coronation Street* and *Eastenders*, or to the triumphal trumpets and distorted electric guitars of *The A-Team* signature tune. Fans of the big screen in the UK have opted to say farewell while their guests listen to music from *Gladiator*, *The Great Escape*, *633 Squadron* and *The Italian Job.*

We're coming to the boundaries of British idiosyncrasy though with one man's choice of 'The Laughing Policeman' by Charles Penrose, and the man (it had to be a man) who replaced the music at his funeral with the sound of trains being shunted in sidings.

Top ten unsubtle songs for funerals

1. 'The Drugs Don't Work' – The Verve
2. 'Heaven Knows I'm Miserable Now' – The Smiths
3. 'Flying Without Wings' – Westlife
4. 'There She Goes' – The La's
5. 'I Saw Her Again Last Night' – The Mamas and the Papas
6. 'Spirit in the Sky' – Norman Greenbaum
7. 'Keep the Faith' – Bon Jovi
8. 'Cold As Ice' – Foreigner
9. 'Alive and Kicking' – Simple Minds
10. '(Don't Fear) The Reaper' – Blue Oyster Cult

Chapter 14

The Eulogy

Just a few words

Though it's still fairly common for the cleric conducting the funeral to say a few words about the deceased, the trend now is for a member of the family or close friend to deliver the eulogy, even amongst those who still choose religious services. The feeling is that what is said will be truer and more from the heart since modern city living can mean that our local religious rep is unlikely to know us quite as personally as in earlier, less crowded times. Of course the smaller the town or village, the more likely God's local rep will know all about you, and that isn't necessarily a good thing when it comes to eulogies. A more personal pen portrait means that the eulogy doesn't have to be quite so solemn either, not that I'm suggesting that all clerics are by nature solemn – yours might well be one of those with his own guitar who asks you to call him Malcolm.

It's not for everyone of course, only 10 per cent of eulogies in the UK are delivered by those close to the permanently relocated, but if the 50 per cent that now indulge in the US is any indication then the do-it-yourself eulogy is going to be big and soon.

There are no limits to the number of people out there willing to help you if the honour falls on you to say a little something about your mother, father, brother or best friend. There are plenty of books on the subject, mostly written by writers in the US so far, though there is a British guide, *Well Chosen Words,* that had a helping hand in its inception from the Poet Laureate Andrew Motion, who writes eulogies for royal funerals. There are any number of websites willing to offer advice, a eulogy template or indeed their dedicated eulogy-writing services; you just tell them the same things you'd tell your priest, vicar, mullah or rabbi about the deceased, or answer a selection of basic questions and Bob's your dead uncle.

Back in the US there are an increasing number of priests and funeral planners, willing to guide you through the writing process, though not as many as there are script-writing gurus. Funeral planners are kind of like wedding planners; they will guide and provide for you through the whole process from coffin to funeral cake. The thing to remember is that it's more than possible that members of either profession, though willing and able to help, may have their own agenda for doing so. It's the undertaker's job to make sure you don't run on too long and

The Eulogy

hold up the next appointment – time and stiffs are money – and hence may advise brevity, and it's the priest's belief system that means he won't want you to stray too far into what some have called bad best-man-speech territory.

If you decide not to employ the clergy, the professionals or Eulogies R Us and go your own way, then it's still worth sharing out the task, and the responsibility. Relatives and friends of the deceased are a good source of anecdotes and stories about their lives, though perhaps not your Uncle Geoff, whose tales about your father all seem to start with, 'I remember this time me and your dad were so drunk even our teeth felt dizzy ...'

There are a few things to keep in mind for those who do decide to go it alone. The best eulogies are written from the heart and are personal (though not too personal – the gathering might not want to hear how much you miss your wife's smile, sense of humour and humungous breasts). As a rule of thumb, try to steer clear of the actual death itself, unless it was somehow courageous and stands as an example to others. Though perhaps not 'I think there's a lesson here for us all here – that hand feeding carnivores is best left to the professionals.'

The simplest of eulogies is sometimes merely an edited highlights version of the person's life, though in some cases the highlights are harder to recollect than in others.

Remember it always pays to get the facts straight; there's always going to be someone in the room who knows the real story behind that amusing anecdote about your mother and the amateur dramatic society audition for *Sweet Charity*. Do make sure your speech is actually all about the person who's no longer with us and isn't a platform for your own feelings on the life to come, or not to come. Phrases such as 'empty blackness', 'go we know not where' and 'eternal nothingness' are probably better left unsaid.

The modern eulogy seems to owe more to politics than religion; it's all about spin, and a little spin goes a long way. The idea now is to accentuate the positive, bring back memories of the good times, and paint a rosy picture of the deceased. Yes, they had faults but those faults must somehow be turned into virtues in eulogy terms. As comedian Bob Hope said of the fellow comic and legendarily closed-walleted Jack Benny, 'He was stingy to the end. He gave us 80 years, and it wasn't enough.' Not everyone has the team of writers that Hope had nor the delivery, but the lighter and more humorous the words the longer your speech will be recalled.

Of course humour is subjective and it's probably better to stick to funny stories about the horizontal one than try to be funny in your own right. An amusing tale of your best friend's now passed young wife being mistaken for a student at a parent–teacher conference may raise smiles, but saying, 'I know she's dead and all, but lying there all blonde and beautiful, I still would, you know?' probably won't.

There's no need to take public speaking lessons just to deliver a eulogy, though take a tip from those who do speak publicly and write out what you think you want to say first then get someone else to read it through as a bad-taste checker. The thing about bad taste is we don't always know we have it. Would you say, as one US guy did, 'She's in a better place now, though anywhere's got to be better than that apartment she lived in with her 12 cats and no air conditioning'?

The key to any good eulogy is perhaps to take a leaf out of the book of Estonian funeral etiquette and believe that if you can't say something good, it's best not to say it at all. Or, to quote Ronan Keating, 'you say it best, when you say nothing at all.'

Delivery

The first thing to realise if the delivery of the eulogy is down to you is that a funeral party are not normally a tough audience. They're usually on your side, unless you're giving a eulogy for a dead film, TV or theatre critic, in which case the place will be filled with his/her peers and they'll rip you to shreds afterwards.

And In The End

Even though you know that you're only really talking to family and friends it's best to try to relax before you 'go on'. There are many techniques for chilling before saying your piece, though perhaps not the traditional stiff drink. And in this case the well-worn adage of imagining your audience naked is equally as inappropriate. It's good to have a friend primed and ready to take over, should you need backup. Or indeed do as some now do and get your buddy to duet the eulogy with you. And while two can be company, three or more is close to a Greek chorus and is just getting silly (anyway they won't all be able to find room behind the podium).

Some people choose to have the whole speech printed out for themselves to read from, some choose to use cue cards and yet others happily extemporise, although the latter is best left to those well versed in thinking on their feet: lawyers, car salesmen, con men and comedy club veterans, otherwise you may find that, 'Well ... what can I say about Tony?' is all you end up saying.

Try to remain still and calm; find something to do with your hands, but do not under any circumstances put them into your pockets, especially your trouser pockets if you are a man. Nervousness can lead you to do all kinds of things you wouldn't normally do in public. Finally it's probably best not to make eye contact but to find a fixed spot somewhere in the room to look at, though not the coffin.

Choose anything but the audience, particularly if the cousin who's now suddenly all grown-up and really hot is sitting in the front row, especially if you've actually decided to go with the 'imagine your audience naked' ploy.

In your own words

If you're the one dying you don't have to trust to fate who gets to deliver your eulogy; nowadays the prospective stiff frequently chooses their own grand eulogiser, either personally or by means of their will and testament. This choice is not one to be arrived at lightly though, believe me. Great care needs to be taken, especially if your final decision is to ask your ex-wife. I mean, why would you? We're not all Sonny Bono and our ex-wives are not all Cher.

A better option, and an increasingly selected one, is to write your own eulogy and have it read out for you. It's a good way to humble yourself or aggrandise yourself depending on if you believe in the age-old *bona mors* or not. It's also an excellent way to get certain things off your chest; one Mr Douglas Perryman of Oklahoma ended his with the sentiment, 'Let's not be too critical of the tobacco industry, after all, they did give us a cure for old age.'

It could be a symptom of the modern obsession with self, but the self-penned eulogy is seen as perhaps our last chance to be that other modern obsession – someone. And if you're going to write it yourself then why not deliver it yourself? I'm not talking about from beyond the grave (though that would be a neat trick); the idea is to use the available technology. The 'in their own words' is now the eulogy of choice for many Americans who record their final thoughts to those they expect to be present as an audio tape or onto a digital source, or for those who want to be seen as well as heard, onto video tape, DVD disc or minidisc to be played at the funeral. No doubt the more crematoria and chapels that equip themselves with the technology to deliver such tapes, the more popular the practice will become. After all, who doesn't want to have the last word?

Share the burden

Some people are, unknowingly or otherwise, taking a lead from the Choctaw Native American peoples who perform what they call a 'Funeral Cry'. The ceremony involves sitting in a circle and, starting with the oldest male relative of the deceased, talking about all the good things about the person. The sharing of memories is now quite commonplace in the western world. The safer, and perhaps less stressful, option is, after consulting the family, to write down a list of all the person's good qualities and have them read out at the service.

In the UK as well as the US, another form of communal eulogising is on the rise, the vox pop, where members of the funeral party are invited to step up to the microphone, should one be provided, to say a little something about the deceased. It allows for a shared outpouring of feelings for the principal guest, it allows the mourners to feel as one, but beware – it also allows people to get carried away. Tales from both sides of the Atlantic attest to the fact that once the mike is out there it can be hard to get it back. Sometimes what starts out as a sharing of our thoughts on the life of a man well loved by his family and well liked by his friends can turn into a tirade against a scumbag who only cared for himself and would sell his mother for a dime bag.

Top ten worst possible things said during a eulogy

1. 'I'd like to thank the morticians for keeping true to the spirit of Catherine – she always was a bit heavy on the foundation.'
2. 'Let's not worry so much about where Pete is now, but about his legacy to us, and if anyone wants to come over tomorrow and help me keep the bailiffs out, see me after.'

3. 'Mum's death was a shock to all of us, including her driving instructor.'

4. 'Dad was always trying to teach me stuff, and he was right, it was a really good example of how water and electricity don't mix.'

5. 'Contrary to whatever her ex thinks, I never slept with Susan, but then maybe it's not too late.'

6. 'I always told him there's a right way and a wrong way to do auto-erotic asphyxiation.'

7. 'I know some of you are surprised that I chose to attend, and possibly shocked that I asked to be allowed to speak, but the jury said I was innocent.'

8. 'If there's a message in all of this for us, it's that you can't house-train funnel web spiders.'

9. 'He touched us in so many ways, and in so many places.'

10. 'We're all going to miss him terribly, it's just a pity that the truck didn't.'

Chapter 15
Last Words

There is a knock-on effect of the modern movement towards cremation, or in the case of Germany the rise of the anonymous grave, and that is that the art of the well-wrought epitaph may become entirely a thing of the past. In Britain alone a recent survey found that nearly 50 per cent of those asked would prefer to have a shrub or tree planted in their grave instead of a headstone. And if there's no headstone, there's no epitaph.

The tradition of posting a few words over our grave has been held almost as long as the vast majority of us have been able to read and write; obviously there wouldn't have been much point before. It's not always the above-ground gravestone that bears the inscription, nor is it always a simple message commending the occupier to his or her god. In Japan, for example, it's been the custom to bury two stone tablets with the body, one with the decedent's name and title, the other with a brief biography.

The epitaph was perhaps the first example of people

lightening up about the whole death thing, since, even though the funeral rights may have still been sombre, the words on the headstone began to take on a much wittier tone quite quickly. So maybe it's the writers of these bon mots who were responsible for the whole chucklefest that is many a modern funeral.

Luckily for us, and for this book, there are still people wanting to have the last laugh. There's a village called Sapanta in Northern Romania where the tradition of a few cheery words not only lives on but has also become a tourist attraction. It's okay to laugh aloud in the Sapanta cemetery, where the Patras family have been carving grave markers and adding a poem based on the life of the deceased since the 1930s. A typical example is:

> When I was a young man in the village
> I loved to dance to the sound of the fiddle
> But then I got married
> And my wife wouldn't let me.

The carvings made above the headstone's cross represent the life of the Sapanta resident interred beneath, and the poem on the cross comments on and celebrates that life.

Fame and fortune

It appears that if we are already well known to the world because we're a singer, actor, writer or director, then we only need a few well-selected words to remind our public who we were and make them smile.

The movie director Billy Wilder was the writer and director of the aptly titled *Five Graves to Cairo* and many others, and probably most famous as the director of *Some Like It Hot*. But just in case you didn't know who or what he was, he thought he'd remind you that he wasn't merely a director, thus the words on his stone say 'I'm A Writer'.

Having starred in so many great movies, including Billy Wilder's most famous, the epitaph the great Jack Lemmon left behind was simply:

Jack Lemmon
In

The writer Dorothy Parker lies under a quite subtle 'This One's On Me', while the actress Joan Hackett who never went on any film shoot without a sign for her trailer that read 'Go Away, I'm Sleeping' is now buried with the same instruction for all who come to her grave.

I suppose it helps if you already have a few words forever associated with you, such as the lyrics to a song. It means if you're Dean Martin your gravestone can be inscribed, 'Everybody Loves Somebody Sometime', or if you're fellow rat-packer Francis Albert Sinatra you can rest in peace because 'The Best Is Yet To Come'.

It doesn't have to be the words to a song of course; maybe you're one of the lucky ones who had their own catchphrase, like the voice of Bugs Bunny and a host of other cartoon characters, Mel Blanc. It was probably almost worth dying just to be able to have on the grave:

That's All Folks

There's long been a great literary tradition amongst the inhabitants of the British Isles and it has proven no less so when it comes to their epitaphs. The poet Lord Byron even penned his own little gravestone ditty:

> Posterity will ne'er survey
> A nobler grave than this
> Here lies the bones of Castlereagh
> Stop, traveller, and piss

A more recent example of the famous refusing to take themselves or the world too seriously comes from the grave of the poet, writer and comedian Spike Milligan whose epitaph reads 'Dúirt mé leat go raibh mé breoite', or for those who don't know Gaelic, 'I told you I was ill!'

Happily those of us who lack fame or notoriety in life can sometimes find it after death.

In their own words

The world seems full of those who have chosen to have one final chat with their maker. Thus in a German Cemetery you will find a man who pleads:

> I will awake, oh Christ
> When thou callest me
> But let me sleep a while
> For I am very weary.

Or a wander around a graveyard in Hull, England might acquaint you with one Master Elginbrod:

> Here lies, Master Elginbrod
> Have mercy on my soul, O God
> As I would have if I were God
> And thou were Master Elginbrod.

In Ruidoso, New Mexico you'll find a man who went to his end but never lost his good manners: 'Here lies Johnny

Yeast, Pardon me for not rising.' But then there are always some who want nothing more to do with this world, such as the person buried beneath these words in Vermont, USA: 'I was somebody, who is no business of yours.'

Someone else said

Where the deceased have given no instructions for their own epitaphs the people they leave behind sometimes take it into their own hands to provide one. It might be the choice of the grieving relatives, the community as a whole or sometimes merely that of the craftsman given the task of providing the headstone. Whoever does the choosing, sometimes the words don't always come out the way they were intended. And, boy, are there some fine examples. Let's pop back to Vermont for a start:

> She lived with her husband for 50 years
> And died in the confident hope of a better life.

Or how about the English widow who had inscribed the loving words: 'Rest in Peace, Until We Meet Again.' on her husband's headstone?

The humour at the occupant's expense isn't always accidental, however, and the survivors often can't help but comment on the deceased. The grave of a spinster post-mistress tells us that she has been 'Returned – Unopened', or in a similar, if less blunt, vein there's the lamentation on a London grave that 'Here lies Ann Mann, who lived an old maid, but died an old Mann'. And just in case you thought men were exempt from an after-burial dig, a grave in Ravlunda, Sweden informs us:

> Here beneath rest the ashes of a man who was in the habit
> Of always postponing everything till the day after.
> However, at last he improved and really died Jan 31 1972.

There's at least some sort of a backhanded compliment intended in the epitaph from a grave in England that reads:

> Sir John Strange
> Here lies an honest lawyer;
> And that is strange.

Though I'm not sure if 'Here lies Ezekiel Aikle, aged 102. The Good Die Young' in Atlanta, Georgia was meant to be taken at face value or not.

And then there are those who can't resist getting their 'own back', such as the author from Niagara Falls, Canada who wrote, 'Gone, but not forgiven', or the obviously disappointed heirs of the occupant of a crypt in the New

Church, Amsterdam who had 'Effen nyt', or 'Exactly nothing', engraved on his stone.

Good for business

One man's death is occasionally another man's advertising hoarding, as witnessed by these two examples from the US:

> Here lies Jane Smith
> Wife of Thomas Smith Marble Cutter
> This monument erected
> By her husband
> As a tribute
> To her memory.
> Monuments to this style
> Are 250 dollars

And

> Sacred to the remains of Jonathan Thompson
> A pious Christian and affectionate husband
> His disconsolate widow
> Continues to carry on his grocery business
> At the old stand on Main Street:
> Cheapest and best prices in town.

Last Words

Bereaved Americans were not only aware of the commercial possibilities of the space above the grave but, in an age long before Internet, TV Channel and speed dating, they were also ready for the opportunities for a little personal advertisement. For example, one widow marked her husband's place of rest with:

> Sacred to the memory of
> My husband John Barnes
> Who died January 3, 1803
> His comely young widow, aged 23, has
> Many qualifications of a good wife, and
> Yearns to be comforted.

Yes, they were examples from a long time past and we'd never consider doing anything like it today, would we? Or would we? A video games company actually considered renting out space on gravestones to advertise its latest Playstation shoot-'em-up game. I don't know if was merely a good piece of publicity or if anyone actually signed up their dead relative's gravestone, but it can only be a matter of time before someone cashes in on the possibility of selling gravestone space. If you think about it, those gravestones with the LCD screen are crying out to have adverts in between the personal messages from the deceased. Actually, I thought of it first so back off!

What a way to go

One of the most common non-religious gravestone inscriptions describes the way in which the occupant left this world, and in the US, at any rate, it seems to have had its genesis in the time of the frontier cowboy.

> Here lies a man named Zeke
> Second fastest draw in Cripple Creek.

The sad ending of a Wells Fargo station agent is neatly summed up by the epitaph on his grave in Boot Hill, Tombstone, Arizona: 'Here Lies Lester Moore, Four slugs from a .44, No Les No More.' While in Silver City, Nevada the grave of yet another gunfighter informs us that:

> Here lies Butch
> We planted him raw
> He was quick on the trigger
> But slow on the draw.

We've all watched the odd western movie in our time and we know that where there are cowboys, there are dance halls and dance hall girls such as, 'Toothless Nell (Alice Chambers), Killed 1876 in a Dance Hall brawl, her last words: "Circumstances led me to this end."'A little

further east, and much colder, is Uniontown, Pennsylvania where 'Julia Newton, Died of thin shoes, April
17th, 1839, aged 19 years'. The same town did for the
late Ellen Shannon:

> Who was fatally burned
> March 21, 1870
> By the explosion of a lamp
> Filled with 'R E Danforth's
> Non-Explosive Burning Fluid'.

At around the same time on the other side of the Atlantic Ocean the British seem to have been equally fond of
declaring the mode of death of the grave's occupant.

> Sacred to the memory of
> Major James Brush, Royal Artillery
> Who was killed by the accidental discharge
> Of a pistol by his orderly
> 14th April 1831
> Well done, good and faithful servant.

In the US the 'how' epitaph lingered long into the 20th
century, and it seems to have been a popular form of entertainment in Pennsylvania especially.

> Here lies the body
> Of Jonathan Blake
> Stepped on the gas
> Instead of the brake.

And finally a timely word of warning from the Epitaph of Harry Edsel Smith of Albany, New York:

> Born 1903 – Died 1942
> Looked up the elevator shaft to see if
> The car was coming down.
> It was.

Top ten epitaphs

1. *For Robert Shaw:* If you've watched *Jaws* you'll get the reference and if not you've probably heard something similar somewhere before. These words can be found in East Dalhousie Cemetery, Nova Scotia, Canada: 'Here lies the body of poor Aunt Charlotte/Born a virgin, died a harlot/For 16 years she kept her virginity/A damn'd long time for this vicinity.'

2. *Sound advice:* Another salutary tale from New Jersey, USA: 'Blown Upward/Out of sight/He sought the leak/By candlelight.'

3. *The old ones are the best:* Just read it: 'Jedediah Goodwin/Auctioneer/Born 1828/Going!/Going!/Gone!/1876'.

4. *Fair comment:* From Thurmont, Maryland, USA: 'Here lies an Atheist/All dressed up/And no place to go'.

5. *Bitter? Me?:* In an English cemetery: 'The children of Isreal wanted bread/And the Lord sent them manna/Old clerk Wallace wanted a wife,/And the Devil sent him Anna.'

6. *Lost chord:* From Gloucestershire, England: 'On the 22nd of June/Jonathan Fiddle/Went out of tune.'

7. *Many a song:* Westwood Memorial Park, Los Angeles, California: 'Sleep with a smile/Sammy Cahn'.

8. *Play on words:* The grave of Owen Moore, London, England: 'Gone away/Owin' more/Than he could pay.'

9. *Enough said:* On the grave of Sir Arthur Conan Doyle, England: 'Steel True, Blade Straight.'

10. *The Magic Kingdom:* This particular epitaph actually makes me envious. In the original Disneyland in California there is a ride called the Haunted Mansion and within its graveyard are many headstones. Now, what if you could have your name and epitaph inscribed on one of those headstones? A doctor from Baton Rouge, Louisiana bid over $37,000 for just that honour in a charity auction. He gets his name and a few personal details inscribed on the piece by Disney engineers and a replica to take home with him. Aren't you just a little bit jealous too?

Chapter 16

There Is Superstition

Unsurprisingly, since death is pretty much a universal horror and since the majority of us believe in some kind of power greater than ourselves, many superstitions have grown around death and the funeral.

Equally, it comes as no big shock that there are literally hundreds of superstitions about portents of death, and strangely enough some of them concern funerals. Most are on the same level as a horoscope in a daily paper – so vague that they have to be true in some small measure at least. For example: if large drops of rain fall there has been a death. Well, given the world's population there's a pretty good chance someone has died somewhere. At the other end of the spectrum, there are those that are unlikely enough that they shouldn't cause too much concern, unless of course they happen to you, such as: if you see 13 white horses at the same time, it won't be long before you're taking a short trip to eternity in a hearse. But come on, you only need to eschew horse races, the odd western movie and avoid taking your holidays in the Camargue, and you'll be fine. This leads us to the really obscure kind; a person who re-plants a cedar tree will bite the dust when the lower branches have reached the same height as that person's coffin. What?

Then there are superstitions that deal directly with the ill-effects of the funeral itself; don't ever point at a funeral procession because apparently you'll get yours within a month. It's equally bad luck, those less fatal, to count the cars in a funeral cortège or to meet one head on. If you do, it's down to you to turn round and a make like a tree and leave. It's pretty easy to work out the origins of these: funeral etiquette. My mother always told me it was rude to point and the latter warning no doubt springs from a time when the right of the way of the funeral procession was being less, rather than more, observed and something had to be done. It probably harks back to a time when funerals were so frequent that good old familiarity really did breed contempt. The warning against work on the day of the funeral in many parts of the world is probably another means of enforcing reverence.

A fairly universal superstition concerns the day and date assigned to the funeral. It seems that religious festivals and holidays are pretty much a no-no. And if only it were that simple, since it seems that worldwide there's a real downer on Mondays and Wednesdays, though if you really don't want to put yourself at risk you should totally avoid Friday. Some cultures even suggest a burial on a Friday will lead to another death in the family within a year. Though given the size of the extended family in bygone times, and, when added to the 'six degrees of separation' factor, well, their odds would have been better than most bookies would give you. Oh, and whichever day you do choose, you should tell the bees about the passing. Yes, it's a Euro thing and you'll have to work it out for yourself. Moreover, some say we should stop the clocks until after the service is over, if only so we can't tell how much time the eulogy's spent dragging on and on and on and …

Since we first started disposing of our dead by any other means than pure chance, the human race has constantly written and re-written its rules concerning how to do it. Part of being human is to invent rules to control our lives instead of acting merely on instinct; it's what separates us from the beasts, and from living in supermarkets piled high with our dead uncles. So it must be that superstitions concerning the interment of our dead are warnings of the consequences should we break those rules.

What rules, you cry? Well, firstly there's that whole being afraid of ghosts thing where there are strictures (from the North American Navajos to the banks of the Amazon, to the centre of Africa and beyond) that lead to the burning or pulling down of the deceased's house so that its spirit will have nowhere to go home to and thus be unable to haunt the living. Coincidentally it's a superstition that seemed to die out in cultures who had moved on to more substantial brick buildings. Those who live in houses not scheduled for demolition are frequently required to cover up the mirrors lest the next person who checks himself out will check out.

A quick warning to those of you who read the section on building your own coffin – there are some societies who think that any unused wood must be burned or buried with the body or it will bring you bad luck. Equal bad luck will also befall those who do not abide by the death dress code, especially in Eastern Europe. Knots and hems have been banned from funeral clothes, as has the doing-up of buttons and laces on the decedent. I guess they stop the soul from ascending.

Another European superstition tells us that a woman we bury in black will return to haunt us, but probably only if it's last season's unflattering cut, I'm thinking. And if by any chance we forget to close her eyes she'll look for someone to take with her.

Transport of the dead has its own peccadilloes. It's almost universal to leave the home feet first, just ask any western bad guy, and in many cultures, including the Irish, superstition has it that, in order to let Heaven know you're coming, the coffin should be knocked against the door and the wall of any church along your route. In some cities of the world the number of churches passed and hence amount of knocking could be enough to wake the dead.

There does seem to be a touch of conflict when it comes to whether to shut and lock your doors after the coffin has left the building. Some, the security conscious, say you should, and some, possibly the burglars, say it's bad luck if you do. Though once you get to the graveyard the no-no about not burying the body face down is practically a global thing, with the added superstition in some areas that says if the dead is a first-born infant it will cause that family to be barren from then on. I'm not sure if this comes under the heading of unusual means of birth control or not.

And I can see that the age-old idea that pregnant women shouldn't attend funerals might have something to do with the cycle of life and will probably find some sympathy among modern women, but the superstition that says they shouldn't wear new clothes – it's never going to happen.

And I don't want to start a stampede at the end of the interment but the Georgians and Greeks once believed that the last person to leave the graveside was next on the list, though the Estonians merely believed the last person brought the dead along with them. And talking of stampedes, there are countries, for instance Ireland, where the belief was that the last one in the ground was responsible for watching over the graveyard until relieved by the next interred soul, so you can image the possible indecorous dash should two funerals arrive at the cemetery simultaneously.

Once the grave has been left to its own devices a fairly common thought is that flowers would grow on the grave if the occupants had been good and weeds would grow if they had not, or if the gardener was lazy.

It's not all doom and gloom in the world of the superstitious, however, so let's end this chapter with a couple of examples. For one, much of the world believes that kissing the dead will afford the kisser a long and happy life, not counting the possible years in therapy. And from Ireland here's another of the world's cures for warts: you simply have to toss a handful of earth from under your right foot in front of a funeral procession. Remember: in front of, not at.

Top ten superstitions for this millennium

1. If you hear a gunshot it probably means someone is going to die.
2. It's bad luck to let your wife organise your funeral before you plan on dying.
3. Ordering the funeral feast from a firm that only has a mobile phone number means there'll be a death in the mourning party.

4. Kissing the deceased for any more than a nanosecond can lead to divorce, police involvement or your own website.

5. Unless you're the chief mourner it's bad luck to walk in front of a hearse.

6. Touching wood for good luck doesn't apply to coffins.

7. It's bad luck to hit on the deceased's daughter when her weight-lifter brother is watching.

8. Red sky at night means you forget to check the battery in your smoke alarm.

9. Chain e-mails cannot kill you, but they can empty your bank account.

10. Waking up with a dead person can ruin your career, especially if they were not actually alive when you went to bed with them.

Chapter 17
They Think It's All Over

We're coming to the end of our meander along the highways and byways of man's final journey, though we haven't quite reached the end of the road. The finishing of the funeral service doesn't always signal the end of the festivities or the mourning. Some funeral arrangements include placing food and drink in the house of the deceased or on his grave for up to 40 days after the main event. The Algonkian peoples of Canada used to light a fire on the grave for four days to guide the soul on its final journey, and the Patagonians would slaughter a horse at the graveside so the deceased could giddy up into the next life.

In fact, the tradition of ancestor worship or reverence for the dead is so ingrained in our psyche that, whether cremated, buried or cast upon the waves, we still feel a connection with our dead and strive to maintain that connection. Some of us more so than others: check out the Internet.

You will visit, won't you?

By and large the tradition in the West is to pop along to the graveyard or garden of remembrance armed with a bunch of flowers, exchange a few words with the deceased and the duty's been done. Mostly it's a one-way conversation, more of a monologue actually, but not always. In the East food takes the place of flowers because the dead can't eat flowers. There was a time when tubes were left in the ground leading to the coffin so that food and drink could be provided for the souls down there.

Should your loved one have opted to become part of the land at one of the natural or green burial sites, knowing where to actually lay your flowers might be a little more problematic. It the UK it's not unusual to inter the dead next to a tree that can be marked in a suitably, and eco-friendly, manner. In the US such sites are extensively mapped out, and in the case of a site in Tennessee, USA global positioning satellite technology is used to pinpoint the grave exactly.

Not everyone in the world is quite so perfunctory in the paying of their dues to the dead. The Romans and Chinese both feasted with the dead believing them to need nourishment, and today in modern Italy the graveyards are treated somewhat like parks where families hold picnics with their dead, while the Parisians frequently do lunch with

the deceased. The US natural burial grounds have trail sys-
tems to encourage family outings to visit Granny. In some
countries it is almost as if the living have season tickets to
visit the dead and if you're going to be a regular visitor
then a little extra comfort wouldn't go amiss. In Norway
they sometimes have seats installed to allow the guests of
the dead to sit and chat awhile. However, some people
want seating that's a touch more personal; one widow from
Pittsburgh, USA bought seats from the old Three Rivers
Stadium, home of the Steelers American football team and
the Pirates baseball team, when they were auctioned off.
Her late husband had been a ticket holder for over 40 years
and so she thought it a fitting tribute and an ideal place to
sit with her son for their graveside visits.

The idea of combining comfort for the family of the
deceased with some kind of tribute is spreading, with
memorial benches and prayer stones. I've even been
told unconfirmed stories of not only a bus shelter being
erected over the grave of an ex-bus driver but the grave
of a golf addict having a single putting hole created
above him.

The commercial world hasn't been slow to spot a potential market in the regular visitor to the graveside and in the
US it's now possible to buy a special headstone cleaning
spray guaranteed to remove grime and bird droppings. For
those who wish to visit the grave at night, though why you

would I don't know, a company will supply you with a solar candle that once charged will cast its light for up to 60 hours and comes in both Christian and Jewish format.

A Santiago cemetery in Chile has opened a café with tables overlooking the graves to cater for visitors to the dead. They provide Internet access and a crèche for the kids so you can get a little peace while you visit those who are resting in peace. And just to add an additional crowd draw they have classical concerts and art exhibitions.

Of course not everyone is so keen on spending their living years hanging with the passed. Which is why one man from Chester Jewish Cemetery in England had an automatic teller machine, or cash machine, installed in his headstone and his 25 relatives issued with cash cards. It meant that the only way they could receive their inheritance was to visit him and type in their PIN.

Time to paaaarrrtty!

The sure-fire way to guarantee you get a little attention if you're dead, apart from the whole returning from the grave or haunting gig, is to live in a country that has a tradition of partying with you. And they are many.

In Ghana they have a get-together on the seventh anniversary of the death, with dancing and feasting almost as extravagant as at the original funeral. If you don't want to have to wait quite so long as seven years then you could always die in one of the countries where they have an annual day of the dead or have a party planned for your annual deathday. In Italy your anniversary is celebrated with votive candles and photographs placed around your grave. In Jamaica, 5 February, Bob Marley's birthday, is a national holiday and a concert takes place on a permanent stage built behind his tomb, while in Bulgaria you don't have to be dead famous, just dead, to join in the feast on Palm Sunday; they'll even let you have the leftovers.

Many countries celebrate a day of the dead, and it's normally around the end of October or the beginning of November. The Hindus, Peruvians, Pacific islanders, Native Australians and peoples of Northern Europe all party with the deceased. Food and drink are common to most of the parties. The Corsicans serve bread and wine, and during the Qing Ming festival in China the graves of the ancestors are swept and cakes and fruit are offered. During the Mexican day of the dead the cadavers get to come out and play; well, at least their bones do as they are taken out of their wooden boxes, polished and put on display before they are treated to their favourite food, a sing-song, candlelight, tamales and little skulls made of sugar. Maybe it's not so bad being dead after all: if you die in Taiwan you even get your bones cleaned. When a feng shui master feels the time is right the body is exhumed and the bones stripped of any remaining gooey stuff, before being painted with red ink, wrapped in bamboo paper and reburied after a feast, which includes fruit, biscuits and gifts of flowers and money.

But if you really want to party on after death there's really only one place to be: Samegrelo, Georgia where the dead are as important as the living. The residents of Samegrelo don't bother with waiting for an anniversary to get down with the dead; any time is party time. The living will talk with, sing with, and buy gifts for, the dead. And to make sure they are totally involved in the celebrations a funnel is pushed into the grave for the delivery of wine. If the deceased feels like a cigarette one is lit for them. Well, it's hardly going to kill them now is it?

Cyber mourning

The one thing the modern body has to worry about is the World Wide Web. It may only be happening in a handful of places at this moment but the opportunity to visit a graveyard over the net without having to be there in person must be a worry. The Wadi-a-Hussain graveyard in Karachi, Pakistan offers you the opportunity to make a streamed visit, send virtual flowers and condolences, all without leaving your laptop. Similar services are available in China, Argentina, Australia and England. The Argentin-ian site allows you to interact with the deceased by way of multimedia voiceware, video and messaging.

Elsewhere around the world sites are springing up that offer you the chance to set up an individual memorial page for your eternally re-located loved one where people can leave messages, condolences and in some way offer the dead a touch of immortality through their appearance in search engines.

So before you move on to consider your own options for the funeral fun possibilities possessed by the human race, you might like to consider a future where eventually we'll all be able to take part in the whole process in cyber-space. Who knows, one day we might even be able to die virtually.

Top ten reasons for hanging out in a graveyard

1. *Do you come here often?*: Guys, just hear me out, a grave-yard is the ideal place to pick up the ladies. All you need to do is check the name on the gravestone to make sure they're the widow, turn up with a bunch of flowers of your own and you have an instant chat up line: 'Do you miss him?' Followed by a 'me too, terribly'.

2. *Yes, do you?:* And not to be left out, ladies, the grave-yard might just be the right place to meet eligible men. Firstly, you get to come over all vulnerable and you know how men melt at that, and secondly how far wrong can you go with a guy who's not afraid to show his vulnerable side by crying?

3. *Cyber tears:* Another way of meeting the opposite sex is to check out the cyber mourning sites now proliferating on the net. It's an unofficial dating chat room where you get to look sensitive, not desperate.

4. *Down to business:* The current fad for placing mementos on the grave of our relations means you can find some really cool stuff to re-sell on e-bay.

5. *Sex:* Oh come on, there's plenty of flat places, you're unlikely to be disturbed and being that close to death has got to make you seize every moment you have left.

6. *I'm bored:* If it's only the second week of their summer holidays and your kids are already driving you up the walls, take them to the graveyard to play the alphabet game with the names on the grave stones. The first to get to z gets to not spend the night there.

7. *Drink on me:* I don't know why, but if you're a drunk then graveyards seems to be a choice place to chug it down, maybe because nobody there is being judgemental.

8. *Good exercise:* Graveyards are a cool place for your early morning run; they're quiet, you have many different

routes and there's no traffic, and even when there is it's going so slowly you can probably outrun it.

9. *You never know:* My own personal reason? I live in hope that one day I might meet Buffy.

10. *Sequel:* If you hang around graveyards long enough reading epitaphs, watching funerals and trying out graves for fit and comfort you might end up writing a book like this one. See Mum, I didn't misspend my youth!

Chapter 18

Be Prepared:
Your Own Funeral

It's a good motto to 'be prepared'. And in our time there's no excuse not to be – prepared for your funeral that is, not for death, obviously. It's possible to take total charge of your own funeral arrangements long before the grim reaper turns the corner into your street. Of course, you could leave your final disposition to the whims of your surviving family. It depends how much you trust them and how well you get on with them. Yes exactly, it's best to pay upfront and set out now exactly the where and how. The when is, for the most part, out of your hands.

If you do actually want to be prepared for any eventuality then a Chelmsford, England undertaker now provides a DNA sampling service for those about to be cremated, just in case questions of hereditary disease or possibly paternity issues arise.

For those who don't know where to start, or whether they can indeed have the type of funeral they or their loved one wants, then you can seek advice from a Canadian Natural Death Care Society, who offer advice on caskets, care, transport and ceremonies. Taking it one step further, natural death centres in Australia and Great Britain and a funeral guru in California all hold one-day seminars on taking charge of the burial, giving advice on getting the body home, corpse bathing and the amount of ice, or frozen vegetables, needed to keep the body fresh. If you live in the US it might be worth placing the whole thing into the hands of one of the growing number of funeral planners, who will take the load off and let you put your feet up while they handle everything from booking the band to decorating the mausoleum. You'll find them in many major cities, but beware of wedding planners doing a bit of moonlighting; you don't want the corpse's father being asked to raise a toast.

That said, the world in general normally takes less of a 'hands on' approach and when arranging a funeral most opt for the more usual choice of hiring an undertaker or funeral director. The firm chosen can take various forms, from the huge national chains in the US to the part-time one-man bands in Britain, who may be ambulance drivers or ploughmen by trade. In Marbella in Spain you can even have your last mile presided over by a former beauty queen and Miss World organiser, or if you live in London and want a green funeral you may find yourself in the hands of the sister of British Hollywood actress Amanda Donahoe: Cordelia. If you happen to live in suburban Chicago, USA, when you've finalised the arrangements for your loved one you can pop downstairs to the basement for a game of funeral-themed crazy golf and try to make par over the coffin and gravestone version of Amen Corner at Augusta. It does pay to take care with your choice however, as the cheapest way isn't always the best way to go, as one family of travellers found out when the coffin they had been sold by their undertaker fell apart as they beared its pall due to cheap, flimsy wood.

More and more funeral directors these days sell pre-paid funerals. For a fixed fee you can choose your own coffin, your own final outfit and your own service: the music, the prayers, the location. All your worries about how you might be treated after you're gone can be signed away for one up-front payment, or several reasonable instalments, if you wish. No longer will you need have nightmares about being seen dead in those shoes you swore you wouldn't be seen dead in. No longer will you have cold sweats about that no-good son-in-law of yours tipping the organist to play 'Ding dong, the witch is dead' as you're carried down the aisle. And no more will you have to demand your husband promise he won't pop down to the furnace room afterwards to ask for the coffin back coz he can't see the point in wasting a perfectly good piece of mahogany.

And there are the financial benefits to be considered; the sooner you make your arrangements, the more inflation eats into the undertaker's profits. Given that the average US funeral is said to cost anything from $7,000 to $15,000 and the industry is worth over $16 billion a year, it's got to make sense to let inflation take away some of the pain. It's also something that you might consider if you live in Ghana or Sulawesi Island, Indonesia where it's not uncommon for the body to be stored for six months or more in the case of the former, or up to three years for the latter, in order to save up enough for the elaborate funeral party.

Finally there's the guilt trip you can lay on your family: 'No, no, I've made my own arrangements, and it's all paid for. I don't want to be a burden to anyone.' It's a win-win situation.

Something else you might like to consider doing before you actually hit the dirt is letting people know you're dead. We might have got over that in-your-face funeral thing, with sacrificing slaves and mile-long processions, but most of us would still like an audience when we make our exit.

The most common form of announcement is still the funeral notice in the local or national press. You know the kind of thing I mean; they usually contains such phrases as 'after a short illness', 'after an even shorter affair with his secretary', 'died suddenly' (if you don't count the 30 years he smoked) or 'passed away after a brave fight' (with three prison officers, four other inmates and the chaplain). These skimpy details are then followed by the date, time and location of the funeral. English comic actor and star of *Dad's Army* John le Mesurier announced in *The Times* that he had 'conked out'.

In China distant friends and relatives are sent an announcement of death, which also happens to inform those left behind that it's obviously their fault for allowing the deceased to get that way. This is accompanied by a 'sad report' that details the particulars of the death and the illness, including how the illness started and what medicines were taken for it. Strangely enough a letter containing money towards the funeral expense usually arrives by return of post.

The famous and the infamous will have their passing announced for them, but we can't all expect our death details to be broadcast on television, unless we happen to live in Samegrelo, Georgia. The local cable TV station has a show dedicated to such announcements. It's called 'The Dead Zone'. No, not really.

You may not rate 30 seconds on the local news but you do have alternatives. Thanks to new technology, you can arrange for an e-mail to be sent to a list of people you've chosen, informing them of your death. A website has been launched in New Zealand that sends out the message when it is activated by someone you have entrusted with the code. Unless they die before you of course – so it's best to choose someone younger and fitter than yourself.

Be Prepared: Your Own Funeral

In Spain and in Texas similar services also allow you to add video clips and photographs. Your buddies can even get back to you by sending an e-card of sympathy or SympathE-card.

Okay, so it's all a bit spooky and 'if you're watching this then it means I'm dead' thrillerish, but it's also quite a cool idea when you think about it. It takes away the burden from your family of having to contact everyone in your address book and give them the bad news. It also means you get to write your own message, in your own words: 'Hello, if you're reading this e-mail, then I have (delete as required: passed on, died, shuffled off this mortal coil, kicked the bucket, gone to meet my maker, checked out, bit the big one, cashed in my chips, reached my journey's end, left the building forever, assumed room temperature, or given up oxygen).'

It's probably not such a good idea to put your close relatives on the list, though I think it's perfectly fine for those acquaintances you see rarely, and now even more rarely. You can even get even by writing that message you always wanted to send to your boss, your ex-wife or your bank manager, safe in the knowledge that it'll be sent only after you're dead and they've got no comeback. You really will, at last, have the final word.

And just in case you get blocked as spam, or the PC's filter decides you're porn, it can't be long until someone provides a similar service by text message: 'SRY 2 TELL U SHAZ AS BIT DE BIG 1'.

While we're on the subject of the use of modern technology, you might also like to think about making a video will. They are not for everyone, and not particularly widespread yet, but they have the virtue of combining a last goodbye with the ability to make sure that your wife gets what's coming to her.

It's your funeral, so why wait?

There is one other thing you can do before you go – have your funeral. It's called a Living Funeral and is *the* thing to do. It's like a regular funeral, only you're there. Well, of course you're there during a regular funeral, but only in body, not in mind or spirit. Obviously there are bound to be other differences from a normal funeral; you won't want things to go quite so far, it should wind down before they get around to the actual burial or cremating part (just in case, it's probably not such a great idea to have too much booze at your awake wake).

The good thing about these living funerals is that you get to plan them yourself, kind of like the pre-paid funerals previously mentioned; the difference is you get the benefit.

Be Prepared: Your Own Funeral

Why not invite your friends to your favourite watering hole, lie back – in a coffin if you wish, but it's not mandatory – and listen to them say all the nice things about you that you would have missed at your real funeral. You don't have to be quite as formal as Jos Thys from Belgium who had his living funeral as a birthday present and did the whole wreath-laying, black-wearing, eulogy-giving thing. Why not lighten up and have a themed living funeral? If the time of your life was the 70s then have a 70s funeral, or a *Saturday Night Fever* funeral or a *Star Wars* funeral – let your imagination run riot. You only die once, so do it with style.

The terminally ill Hungarian theatre director Péter Halász decided he'd lie in state for a week so that people could pay their last respects before he died. He lay in a coffin in a Budapest art gallery to allow people to view the body. Obviously it was an open coffin viewing.

Perhaps the ultimate in attending your own funeral is to have yourself buried piecemeal like one Antonio Magistro from Sicily who had his amputated foot interred in a coffin after a short service, though he has no plans to join it anytime soon.

And just in case this book has actually inspired you to start thinking about making arrangements for your own funeral, living or otherwise, here is a tick list for you to plan your own way to go. All you have to do is add your own taste, or lack of.

Your own funeral template

1. *When I die I wish the following people to be notified:*

_____   _____

_____   _____

_____   _____

_____   _____

_____   _____

by:

a) Newspaper ☐

b) Text ☐

c) E-mail ☐

d) Town Cryer ☐

2. *I wish to be buried, and my coffin should be:*

a) Eco-friendly and made of: _____

b) Home-made by me ☐

c) Home-made by: _____

d) Rented ☐

e) Purchased from: _____

and made of: _____

f) The lining should be: _____

g) Shaped like: _____

h) Other: _____

3. *I wish to be buried in the following clothes/outfit:*

_____

_____

4. *I wish to buried:*

a) In the following graveyard:

_____

b) In my own garden ☐

c) In the garden of: _____

d) At the following location:

_____

e) At the green burial site at:

_____

f) At sea ☐

g) Other: _____

5. *I wish to be buried:*

a) Standing up ☐

b) Sitting down ☐

c) Horizontal ☐

d) Perpendicular ☐

e) Facing the following direction:

_____

f) Other: _____

6. *I wish to take the following with me:*

_____

7. *I wish to be cremated:*

    a) At the following crematorium:

_____

    b) At home   ☐

    c) At the following location:

_____

    d) Other: _____

8. *I wish my ashes to be interred in:*

    a) An urn purchased from:

_____

    b) An urn shaped like: _____

    c) The following household object:

_____

    d) Other: _____

9. *I wish my ashes to be kept:*

    a) In the following columbaria:

_____

    b) In the crypt at: _____

    c) At home, on/in: _____

    d) Other: _____

10. *I wish my ashes to be scattered:*

    a) At the following churchyard/graveyard/
       garden of remembrance:

    _____

    b) At sea   ☐
    c) At home   ☐
    d) In my garden   ☐
    e) Other: _____

11. *I wish my ashes to scattered in the following manner:*

    _____
    _____

12. *I wish my wake to take place in the following location:*

    _____

13. *I would like the following people to attend:*

    _____   _____
    _____   _____
    _____   _____
    _____   _____
    _____   _____

14. *I would like the theme of my wake to be:*

    _____

15. *I would like the following people to speak at my wake:*

_____   _____

_____   _____

_____   _____

16. *I do/do not want flowers.*

17. *I would like a donation made to the following:*

_____

18. *I would like my service to take place at:*

_____

19. *I wish to be transported to the funeral service by:*

_____

20. *I would like the journey to take the following route:*

_____

_____

21. *I would like the following to be my pall-bearers:*

_____   _____

_____   _____

_____   _____

Be Prepared: Your Own Funeral

22. *I would like the following to be part of the service:*

    _____   _____

    _____   _____

    _____   _____

    _____   _____

    _____   _____

23. *I would like the following as a backdrop to the service:*

24. *I wish the eulogy to be read by:*

25. *I would like the following extract/poem read out:*

26. *I would like the following music at my funeral:*

    a) _____

    b) _____

    c) _____

27. *I would like the music played by/on:*

_____

_____

28. *I wish my funeral feast to take place at :*

_____

29. *I wish the following food/drink to be served:*

_____

_____

_____

_____

30. *I would like to have the following as my final resting place:*

    a) Grave without headstone   ☐

    b) Grave with headstone, made of and shaped like the following:

    _____

    c) Crypt, shaped like the following:

    _____

    d) Mausoleum, shaped like the following:

    _____

    e) Tomb, shaped like the following:

    _____

31. *I wish the following to be my epitaph:*

_____

_____

_____

_____

32. *I wish my ashes to be turned into the following:*

_____

33. *I do not wish to be buried/cremated but wish to leave my body to:*

_____

34. *I wish to be frozen.* ☐

35. *Any other special instructions:*

_____

_____

_____

_____

SIGNED _____

DATED _____

WITNESSED _____

About the Author

Like most writers Keith Lindsay has more than a few 'formers' on his CV: teacher, ice cream man, tea lady, shop assistant, performance poet and part-time actor to mention a few. Keith's longest lasting employment so far has been as a scriptwriter with credits on such television shows as *Hale and Pace, Birds of a Feather* and most recently *The Green Green Grass*, John Sullivan's spin off from *Only Fools and Horses*.

Keith was born, and still lives in, the Midlands with his wife Sue and has two offspring, Jamie and Hannah, who both like to think they are all grown up now.